Daughters Who Care

Daughters Who Care

DAUGHTERS CARING FOR MOTHERS AT HOME

Jane Lewis
Barbara Meredith

ROUTLEDGE
London and New York

First published in 1988 by
Routledge
a division of Routledge, Chapman and Hall
11 New Fetter Lane, London EC4P 4EE

Published in the USA by
Routledge
a division of Routledge, Chapman and Hall, Inc.
29 West 35th Street, New York NY 10001

Typeset by Boldface Typesetters, London EC1
Printed in Great Britain at
Biddles, Guildford

British Library Cataloguing in Publication Data

Lewis, Jane
Daughters who care: daughters caring for
mothers at home.
1. Aged women – Home care – Great
Britain 2. Mothers and daughters –
Great Britain
I. Title   II. Meredith, Barbara
362.6'0941   HV1481.G52

ISBN 0–415–00681–3
ISBN 0–415–00682–1 Pbk

Library of Congress Cataloging in Publication Data
Lewis, Jane (Jane E.)
Daughters who care: daughters caring for mothers at
home/Jane Lewis, Barbara Meredith.
p. cm.
Bibliography: p.
Includes index.
ISBN 0–415–00681–3. ISBN 0–415–00682–1 (pbk.)
1. Aged women – Home care – United States. 2.
Parents, Aged – Home care – United State. 3. Mothers
and daughters – United States.
I. Meredith, Barbara. II. Title.
HV1461.L47 1988
649.8 – dc19

Contents

Acknowledgements

The idea for this study emerged out of conversations with a number of people working in the field, to whom I owe a considerable debt. In particular I would like to thank Janet Finch and Clare Ungerson; Sheila Abrams and Dennis Marsden for taking the time to tell me about their own qualitative study of carers; Paul Thompson for making suggestions about the sample and interviewing techniques; and Jill Pitkeathley of the National Council for Carers and their Elderly Dependants and Judith Oliver of the Association of Carers, both of whom gave their enthusiastic support and provided valuable contacts. Professor Margot Jefferys and Peter Willmott were kind enough to read the whole manuscript for me. My largest debt of all is to the women who agreed to be interviewed.

The study could not have been carried out without the financial support provided by the Rockefeller Foundation and I am also indebted to Gus Stewart at the London School of Economics for his care and sympathetic help in administering the grant. Finally I am deeply indebted to the two researchers, Barbara Meredith and Sue Tester, who worked with me on the project. We all three shared the work of interviewing (Barbara Meredith and Sue Tester bearing the brunt) and the crucial early discussions during which we decided how to approach the interpretation of the material. I took responsibility for conceptualising and writing the study. Barbara Meredith shared the work of analysing and discussing the material throughout, took responsibility for the development of Appendix B and contributed to the writing of parts of chapters 1 and 7.

Jane Lewis
London School of Economics

CHAPTER 1

Caring and carers: the issues

The recent burgeoning of literature on the elderly is a product of the latest in a series of waves of anxiety about an ageing population. The immediate post-war period saw a similar rise of concern in the wake of demographic analysis which emphasized the dangers of a falling birth rate and an increasingly unfavourable dependency ratio. The anxiety today focuses not only on dependency ratios and the fear that an ageing population will impose a heavy economic burden, but also on how the elderly are to be cared for and how the costs of their care are to be met.

All developed countries are currently facing the prospect of a rapidly ageing population, and as Parker (1981) has remarked, Britain has one of the oldest populations in the world. In 1981, 15 per cent of the British population was aged over 65, and 6 per cent was aged over 75 (Rossiter and Wicks 1982). Between 1971 and 1981 alone, the number of people aged over 75 – the age group commonly agreed to be in need of most care – increased by 20 per cent, and by the year 2001 the number of over 75s is projected to rise by 30 per cent and of those over 85 to almost double (Ermisch 1983; Wicks and Henwood 1984). Thus both the absolute numbers and the proportions of 'old old' have increased and will do so further. Furthermore, women constitute a larger proportion of both the old and the 'old old'. In 1979, of those aged 75 or over, 66 per cent were female and among the over 85s, this proportion was 76 per cent (Rossiter and Wicks 1982).

A bald statement of demographic trends tends to result in the elderly being labelled a 'problem'. A recent study of the 1950s and 1960s British literature on ageing (Harper and Thane 1986) shows how the elderly were usually described as 'unproductive' members of society and portrayed as doubly burdensome in terms of their poverty and need for care. More recently studies have shown the problem of acute poverty among the elderly to have receded (Atkinson 1984); the overwhelming current pre-occupation is how to care for elderly people who require increasing amounts of help. The problematizing of the elderly as a group is unfortunate. As Clare Wenger (1984: 22) has put it: 'We know far more about the problems of the elderly than we do about their successes and competences.' Only some 6 per cent of over-65s are in institutional care and in 1976 it was estimated that of those in the community, 0.3 per cent were permanently bedfast and 4.2 per cent permanently housebound (Hunt 1978). However, the level of need for assistance on the part of the remainder is extremely varied. The point at issue is how, now and in the future, increasing numbers of frail elderly people may be assisted to remain in the community, where most would prefer to be.

WHO DOES THE CARING?

The number of elderly living with kin has actually fallen dramatically from about 42 per cent in the early 1960s to 20 per cent at the beginning of the 1980s. The 1981 Census shows almost one-third of elderly people living alone, 45 per cent of elderly women and 17 per cent of elderly men. However, Peter Willmott (1986) has suggested that when the proportion of elderly with children living nearby and providing informal care is considered, as many elderly now as a generation ago enjoy informal care, usually by female relatives. Much recent feminist research has made the point that in practice community care means family care and that family care means care by female family members. Indeed the Equal Opportunities Commission estimated in 1982 that there were one and a quarter million female carers in Britain (EOC 1982a and b), while the 1984 Women and Employment Survey found 13 per cent of all women had caring responsibilities for sick or elderly dependants, and more than 20 per cent of women aged 40 or over (Martin and Roberts 1984).

However, recent analysis of the 1980 General Household Survey (GHS) data has provided concrete evidence as to the significant number of households in which care is given to an elderly person by a spouse (Arber *et al.* 1986). Fully 51 per cent of carers are spouses and 26 per cent of them husbands. A further 6 per cent of single children caring for parents are male. From the GHS data it is possible to deduce that 55 per cent of all carers are female, 35 per cent male and in 10 per cent of cases the sex of the carer is unknown. Of the female carers, 45 per cent are spouses, and 35 per cent daughters. This suggests that attention needs to be paid to different types of carers, whose needs and circumstances may vary. Certainly caring by spouses and by single men is an under-researched area, yet the widely shared and persistent expectation that it is daughters who will care signals the need further to consider their role. Hazel Qureshi and Alan Walker's (1988) research shows the existence of a perceived hierarchy of preferred carers with a daughter the firm first choice in the absence of a spouse. Furthermore, the position of daughters as carers is potentially very difficult. They must balance their responsibilities for elderly people with those for husbands and children, and the needs of their families with those of their employers. It also appears that daughters tend to be caring for more highly disabled elderly (certainly more so than are sons); and that daughter carers receive by far the lowest level of community-based services, such as home helps and meals on wheels (Evandrou *et al.* 1986).

In view of the way in which caring has been constructed as preeminently women's work, some attention has been devoted to the future likelihood of women being either unavailable or unwilling to do it. Some ten years ago, Moroney (1976) drew attention to the dwindling numbers of single women, classically assumed, in the manner of the government's 1981 White Paper, *Growing Older*, to be the 'natural' carers of elderly parents (Parliamentary Papers 1981). The ratio of single middle-aged women has declined from 160 per 1,000 elderly people in 1911 to 50 in 1971, a much greater proportion of adult women having married since World War II. It is also the case that the ratio of women aged 45–49 (the typical age range for female carers) has decreased from 850 per 1,000 elderly in 1911 to 490 in 1971. However, in his discussion of demographic trends influencing the family situations of older women, Timaeus (1986) points out that women reaching the age of 65 during the last two decades of this century will be more likely to have children to call on than the cohort who completed their family building before the war. He also assumes that the increased presence of children implies the increased availability of carers, and that it will continue to be primarily daughters who provide co-resident care for those needing it. The implications of a divorce rate of 1 in 4 and of increased geographic mobility are harder to predict. Reconstituted families could conceivably provide an extra source of care, particularly while the elderly person remains at least partially independent.

Perhaps the most uncertain factor in assessing women's future caring role is the change in the pattern of sex roles and in particular changing female employment patterns. During the 1950s, 1960s and early 1970s, married women's typically bipolar work pattern meant that the female carer, usually middle-aged – whom Brody (1981) has called the 'woman in the middle' – tended to have left the workforce to care for children and was also in a position to care for elderly dependants. However recent studies (e.g. Joshi 1984) have shown that women are now showing substantially greater attachment to the workforce, taking breaks only for maternity leave. This behaviour, together with the possibility that feminist arguments regarding the desirability of sharing care more equally in society between men and women might gain more widespread acceptance, has cast doubt over the future of women's traditional caring role. Today's carers grew up in the late 1930s and 1940s and therefore might be expected to have absorbed fairly traditional ideas regarding women's responsibility for caring. However, Brody's (1981; Brody *et al*. 1983) research with three generations of female family members indicates that today's young women also have a very strong commitment to care, as well as a strong preference for equal opportunities in the public sphere, a position which may betoken future conflicts.

WHY DO WOMEN CARE?

Any simple notion that women's increased participation in the public sphere automatically results in a diminution of their caring role is surely misplaced. Perhaps the most striking characteristic of women's experience in the twentieth century has been the way in which they have gained increased access to the public sphere, while retaining full responsibility for domestic labour and the work of caring for other family members. In other words, while women have entered the public sphere in ever-increasing numbers, men have not assumed a more equal share of work in the home. We cannot interpret women's relationship to caring in terms of a series of choices about the proper and rational allocation of time and resources. There is, as Martin Bulmer (1986a: 116) has recognized, the part played by 'complex networks of interdependency involving power relations between and within generations and the sexes'. Women's decision to care is made within a framework of widely held assumptions that caring is women's work and that, in the end, caring should take precedence over other types of work.

In all probability a majority of women want to care and recent research, much of it feminist, has sought to explain why this may be so, in terms both of the patterns of socialization and the structural constraints experienced by women, and of the way in which women have internalized the injunction to care. Hilary Graham (1983) has pointed out the extent to which the caring role provides women with part of their feminine identity; it is more than another species of work. Carol Gilligan (1982) has argued that the feminine personality comes to define itself in relation to and in connection with others more than does the masculine personality, which is defined primarily through separation. In this construction, concern for others rather than self – an ethic of care – becomes central to understanding femininity. Such a concern for others is not necessarily some kind of happy altruism. As Gilligan points out, women may also *judge* themselves by their capacity to care. Thus failure to do so, for whatever reason, commonly induces guilt. In addition, from a materialist perspective, women have a much more limited range of opportunities open to them than do men. Alan Walker (1983: 111) has remarked on the 'close coincidence of status and interest between elderly dependants and the women they depend on'. In other words, carers share a dependent status as a result of their restricted access to the labour market. If this is so, the work of caring, combining as it does labour and love, might appear particularly worthwhile to many women. However, middle-class single women carers, and increasingly married women also, have careers (admittedly in a relatively narrow range of occupations) to which they are committed, which only makes it more difficult to explain the injunction to care that they experience in terms solely of conflict caused by constraints imposed from without.

Willingness to care is usually considered in relation to ties of affection and the pull of obligation. These are certainly powerful motivating forces and the balance between them is often difficult to establish. But Gilligan and Graham are suggesting that the injunction to care is seated more deeply still in the female personality as well as being elicited by a close relationship, usually with kin. We can thus begin to understand why the injunction to care is so powerful and why the approach taken by those who treat the work of caring as simply non-market work that women voluntarily choose for its intrinsic satisfaction is inadequate. Women's willingness to care is considerably more complex than a decision to opt for a labour of love rather than money. It may be as Jean Elshtain (1981) suggests that women consciously decide that the private world of home and family has greater integrity and has more to offer than any other. This view depicts women's willingness to care positively, seeing it as part of an intrinsically female culture and value system that is sometimes represented as being of a higher moral order than that of the public sphere of men.[1]

Recent British feminist literature on caring prefers to draw the conclusion that the caring ethic should become the property of men as well as women (e.g. Finch and Groves 1983). For not all women experience the injunction to care positively. Many experience conflicting demands on their capacity to care – from husbands as well as elderly kin – or tensions between the demands of others and emergent desires for self-fulfilment. Perceived failure to juggle these successfully and thus to fulfil the injunction to care may result in guilt and unhappiness. It is well known that carers are especially prone to use the word 'guilt' to describe their feelings. Indeed, Clare Ungerson (1985) and Hilary Land and Hilary Rose (1985) have suggested that it is very hard to know where the love ends and the guilt or compulsory altruism begins. In other words, there will in all probability be 'costs' to caring, and the extent of these is not easily susceptible to the measures favoured by economists. Certainly it is possible to estimate the amount of income foregone by women who give up work to care, as Nissel and Bonnerjea (1982) have effectively shown. They estimated that the carers in their sample forfeited an average of some £4,000 a year in income by staying at home to care. Carers may feel very bitter about such material losses. They may also nevertheless feel glad that they cared. The strain on their material resources, their own health, and the possible tensions between the work of caring and other aspects of their lives

1 Gilligan (1982) and Elshtain (1981) can both be interpreted in this way, although we would argue that such an interpretation is more questionable in the case of the former than the latter.

has to be balanced against the powerful injunction to care and the guilt if it is ignored.

THE MEANING OF CARING

There have been some admirable recent attempts to draw attention to the labour inherent in the work of caring. Roy Parker (1981) has suggested the use of the word 'tending', which may be broken down into four component parts – duration, intensity, complexity and prognosis.[2] The idea is appealing not least because care can then be measured and costed. The problem, as Graham (1983) has perceived, is that it is not possible to divorce the labour of tending from the feelings of love and the ties of obligation that are part and parcel of the way in which women approach caring. Caring becomes both labour and love because of the way in which the capacity to care for and care about someone else are collapsed, at least in respect to women carers. It is commonly assumed that the one follows 'naturally' from the other. As Dalley (1988) has observed, 'the concentration of multiple functions in the role of mother seems to be at the root of the caring issue'. Beginning with children, it is assumed that because women bear them they will also rear them, whereas a man can be a biological parent and not be expected to care for his child on a day-to-day basis. His natural duty is assumed to be that of provider, not carer. It seems that the identification of caring about with caring for – between love and labour – continues to characterize women's relationships with elderly and infirm dependants.

This is not to deny that there is a need for greater understanding of what might be termed the caring task. Caring for the physically ill presents different problems from caring for the mentally ill and, more important still, carers perceive and experience the various problems of personal care differently. Furthermore, caring has its own sequence and biography. The task changes over time often in response to particular triggers, whether social (such as the elderly person's loss of a spouse), or physical (such as a stroke or a fall). 'Snapshot' studies of carers often miss the way in which the caring task develops, its varying intensity and the changing nature of the burden it represents. An old person may

2 His analysis has been taken up by others, for example Allen *et al.* (1983).

not be very mentally or physically disabled, but he/she may still place substantial restrictions on the carer. But if credence is given to feminist analyses, the meaning of caring becomes additionally complicated. The decision to care may derive from feelings of obligation and affection stemming from the dynamics of kin relationships and from the female carer's sense of feminine identity, in which case the work of caring will involve more than attention to particular identifiable personal needs of the elderly person.

Caring may thus best be approached as an integrated set of relationships and personal caring tasks. During the early phase of care, support may come closest to being described as a network, continuing from the period before the need for care began – the neighbour who pops in and shops or chats performing as great a task as the relative stopping by each week to 'check' on 'x'. With the next 'trigger' in the caring sequence, Qureshi's idea of a 'caring hierarchy' becomes more important than that of a 'network', and in the absence of a spouse a female carer will most often assume the burden of responsibility for, although not necessarily perform, all the caring tasks. The relationship between the primary carer and the elderly person may be seen as central. Feeding into it are the relationships the elderly person is able to sustain with friends, neighbours, and kin; the carer's other home and work-based relationships; and the range of support both are able to draw on from professionals or voluntary organisations. Once caring is conceptualized in this way it then becomes clear that many forms of support are needed – emotional, practical and material – and that their precise content will vary depending on the nature of any particular set of caring relationships. A change in any one variable, for example, an increasing level of dependency of the elderly person on the carer for all forms of support and social interaction, or the increasing isolation of the carer as the burden of care intensifies (as a result of the withdrawal of friends, temporary or permanent retirement from work, or a supportive sibling moving away), may result in a need for additional or a different form of support.

COMMUNITY CARE POLICY

The implications of all this for community care policies are many. Women are willing to care, but not only because it is biologically natural, or because they have simply made a rational choice to do so. Their work of caring will often be accompanied by considerable stress, material, physical, and emotional. Unlike both the earlier literature, which assumed such care to be unproblematic, and recent government policy documents which assume there to be no alternative, much of the recent feminist literature has argued particularly strongly for a reconceptualization of community care so that the burden of caring is more equally shared between the formal, voluntary, and informal sectors, and between the sexes. As a long-term goal, feminists desire to see more men doing caring work within the family and as paid carers, and as a bottom line look for more support from formal and voluntary sectors for the informal supporters of whichever sex. Indeed, as Alan Walker (1986) has remarked, if society were organized round a caring ethic, the work of caring would be better valued and rewarded.

'Supporting the supporters' has recently become a watchword among both academic researchers and practitioners. In particular, the study by Levin, Sinclair and Gorbach (1983) of supporters of the confused elderly has stressed the crucial way in which formal services can act to stop the build-up of strain for carers. The logic of this may seem obvious, but in terms of the history of community care policy the idea of 'sharing the care' between informal supporters and the state in particular is a major departure. Indeed the focus on the importance of community care is itself relatively new. In the work on the needs of the elderly sponsored by the Nuffield Foundation immediately after the war, more attention was paid to institutional provision than anything else (Rowntree 1947 and Sheldon 1948). This was despite the recognition that between 95 and 98 per cent (estimates varied) of the elderly lived independently, but in keeping with the authors' preoccupation with the elderly as an unproductive and dependent group. Similarly the 1948 National Assistance Act had much more to say about residential care than it did about community services. As Means and Smith (1985) have remarked, the late 1940s were distinguished by a singular lack of imagination about forms of care other than residential. This attitude changed during the 1950s and there developed substantial agreement that old people should remain in their homes as long as possible, with Peter Townsend (1957) arguing on grounds of the increased happiness of those elderly enabled to remain at home. The assumption that female family members would provide the supports needed by the elderly was explicit and unquestioned. Means and Smith (1985) cite examples of geriatricians and politicians in the 1950s who expressed the belief that it was part of women's normal role and duty to care for the elderly. Similarly, in acclaiming the family bonds revealed by his study of families in London's East End, Townsend (1957: 194) concluded that people with families, especially daughters, made few claims on the state and that it would therefore be counterproductive 'if the state, through housing and other policies, separated individuals from their kin and thus made more professional services necessary'. No consideration was given to the burden falling on women carers. Indeed, as in other areas of government policy such as income maintenance, government tended to fear that any additional help provided by the state would sap the family's incentive to provide. One reason for the slowness in developing the home help and meals on wheels services lies in the belief that these were areas of support properly confined to the family (Means and Smith 1985).

Government first began to talk seriously about community care in the context of the mentally ill and used the term to refer to services located in the community rather than in institutions (Ayer and Alaszewski 1984; Walker 1986). The mid-1970s saw an attempt to extend the concept of community to include institutions. In particular, the reorganization of the National Health Service (NHS) was intended to promote the integration and rationalization of services in and outside the hospital (Lewis 1986), the motive being twofold: to improve the co-ordination and quality of care and to shift resources from the extensive acute hospital sector to the community in the hope of holding down spiralling hospital costs. As the recent report by the Audit Commission reveals, such a shift in resources never took place and community care policy has been one of muddling through (Audit Commission 1986). Furthermore, when hospital costs continued their inexorable rise, integration of services as a strategy for cost control was abandoned and by the late 1970s and early 1980s government was seeking to limit costs in *all* areas of service delivery. As a result, the meaning of community care shifted once more from care *in* the community – with the elderly person enjoying the support of informal caring networks and community and institutional services as necessary – to care *by* the community, with the emphasis firmly on the role of informal family care.

The 1978 Consultative Document *A Happier Old Age* stressed the importance of family links in old age, while continuing to emphasize the importance of a 'joint approach' to care on the part of formal and informal agencies, recognizing that there might be limits to the community's capacity to care (DHSS and Welsh Office 1978). The 1978 Wolfenden Committee report on the future of voluntary organizations provided firm support for informal and voluntary care: 'We place a high value on this system of care, both because of its intrinsic value and because its replacement by a more institutional form of caring would be intolerably costly' (Wolfenden 1978: 182). The 1981 Government White Paper, *Growing Older*, reflected that government's increasing concern to limit the obligations of the state:

> Whatever level of public expenditure proves practicable, and however it is distributed, the primary sources of support and care for elderly people are informal and voluntary. These spring from the personal ties of kinship, friendship and neighbourhood. They are irreplaceable. It is the role of public authorities to sustain and, where necessary, develop – but never to displace – such support and care. Care *in* the community must increasingly mean care *by* the community.
>
> (P.P. 1981: 3, italics in original)

The document argued that families were best placed to understand and meet the wide variety of personal needs of the elderly person and admitted that this 'may often involve considerable personal sacrifice, particularly where the "family" is one person, often a single woman caring for an elderly relative'. Unlike the literature of the 1950s and 1960s, the burden falling on women was recognized, but women were also being effectively told that they had no alternative but to shoulder it.[3]

In his keynote speech to Directors of Social Services at Buxton in September 1984, the Secretary of State, Norman Fowler, signalled a change in responsibilities of social services departments broadly in tune with this thinking – the aim would be to switch their emphasis from providing services to the task of co-ordinating social care, whether issuing from private, voluntary, informal, or formal sectors (Bulmer 1986b). Such a fundamental reorientation

3 Means and Smith (1985) and Goldberg and Connelly (1982) provide good overviews of policy developments since the war.

has yet to materialize. All too often government documents consider the position of carers only because they represent a cost effective option. For example, noting that carers save government in excess of £3,000 a year per elderly person cared for, the Audit Commission (1985: 43) concluded that 'Carers have needs and rights – since their work is important to the economy of the health and social services.'

As Alan Walker (1986) has suggested, current government strategy rests in large part on the idea that there are untapped sources of informal care which can be called into play to attend to the needs (great and small) of an increasing population of old and very old people. The demographics of the female caring population and the already powerful injunction to care experienced by women makes this a dubious proposition. More volunteer help might be forthcoming (Qureshi, Challis, and Davies 1983), but after a certain point in the caring sequence, when personal care tasks require increasing skill and strength, the part played by voluntary helpers of all kinds becomes secondary and their role tends to be circumscribed. In his address to the annual social services directors' conference (*Guardian*, 20 September 1986), the Secretary of State publicly recognized something first pointed out by Bayley (1973), that a partnership of informal and formal care is crucial and that this might in fact prove more expensive than institutional care. However, the idea of a 'partnership' between the formal and informal sectors has been hard to define and in practice it has proved difficult to construct meaningful links between the two.

More support for the supporters is urgently needed and is being ever more widely canvassed. The issue remains as how best the supporters may be supported? In seeking answers to this question, attention usually focuses on the nature of the personal care tasks that must be performed and the range of services needed to help perform them, often neglecting the circumstances and viewpoints of those directly involved. We would argue that for an extension of community services to be effective, there must be a greater understanding of the nature of the caring relationship. We know very little about the dynamics and dimensions of caring relationships: how the primary caring relationship between carer and person cared for develops over time; how this relationship interacts with other aspects of the lives of the carer and person cared for, for example with friendships or the carer's working life; how real are support networks of kin, friends, neighbours, and voluntary and professional helpers; and how susceptible to breakdown are both they and the primary caring relationship. Greater understanding of caring from the carer's point of view – from the inside out – is crucial if support is to be effective.

AIMS AND METHODOLOGY OF THE STUDY

We decided to focus on the experience of daughters who had cared for their mothers on a co-resident basis. Intergenerational co-resident care is less common than it once was (Wall 1984), not least because of the greater financial capacity on the part of increasing numbers of old and young to sustain separate household units. However, the decision to undertake co-resident care is generally accepted as constituting a fundamental change in the nature of the caring responsibility and is considered by unknown numbers of married women and unmarried children, siblings and other relatives, and spouses. We were particularly interested in explaining the process of identification of the principal carer that goes on prior to the establishment of co-resident care and the subsequent development of the mother/daughter relationship.

We set out to interview daughters who had stopped caring on a co-resident basis, either because their mothers had died or had entered institutions, in order to investigate the legacy of caring: the costs and benefits of caring for the carer, including what Ungerson (1984) has called the uncosted outcomes of care, for example loss of social contacts or poor self-image. Our initial bias was therefore towards the social psychology literature. However, it rapidly became apparent that the interrelated factors in the caring process were complex and required investigation in their own right. In line with our original focus on the central caring relationship between, in the case of this study, mothers and daughters, we attempted to achieve a greater understanding of this relationship and its place in the caring experience. But we also see the research in terms of a pilot study of the dimensions of the caring sequence and the complexity of the matrix of relationships that comprise the caring experience.

Most studies of carers to date have been 'snapshots', focusing on the problems encountered by carers. Some writers (Isaacs *et al.* 1972; Levin *et al.* 1983; Fennell *et al.* 1983; and Arber *et al.* 1986) have acknowledged the importance of assessing the past history of the carer and the elderly person. Arber *et al*. (1986) have stressed the importance of length of period of co-residence in particular, because of the part it plays in generating feelings of obligation and notions of reciprocity, and because of the shifts that take place in the roles of the carer and the elderly person over time. Very occasionally the importance of further investigation into the quality of the central relationship between carer and elderly person and its changes over time has also been raised (Fennell *et al*. 1983). The major task of this study was to develop a method of obtaining, and a vocabulary for describing, what we have called 'caring biographies', and in particular to work out the elements that were crucial to the caring experience, for example, ways of exploring the nature of the central relationship between carer and person cared for. We also set out to locate the development of this central caring relationship in the context of secondary relationships with kin and others at the workplace and in the community to see if we could determine the mixes of experiences and supports over the life course giving rise to particular responses to caring, and more positive or more negative outcomes.

Respondents

All but three of the forty-one respondents had ceased co-resident caring within the last ten years. The exploratory nature of the study and the relatively short timescale justified a non-representative sample and respondents were located via the National Council for Carers and their Elderly Dependants (NCCED), the Association of Carers, a letter to a local newspaper, a Social Services Department of a London borough, the manager of a Part III home, a hospital carers' support group and by personal contact. While respondents could thus be said to be self-referred, twenty-four responded directly to a letter or article in a newspaper or carers' newsletter, and the remainder were indirect referrals, largely from health or social services staff, who had obtained consent in principle from respondents prior to our contacting them. Respondents located through the NCCED were drawn from a number of different English towns, but three-quarters of the sample lived in the home counties.

Almost three-quarters of the respondents were in their fifties and sixties, which we would have expected given that most studies show the typical female carer to be a woman in her fifties (Brody 1981). Twenty-nine were single, nine married, one widowed and one divorced. General Household Survey (GHS) data show more female carers to be married than single (Arber *et al.* 1986). Our sample therefore contained a disproportionate number of single women relative to the population of carers as a whole, due mainly to the fact that half the respondents were located via the NCCED which used to be an organization for single women carers. While in the future there are likely to be fewer never-married carers such as these, the GHS data show that at present single women continue to provide a disproportionate number of carers relative to their numbers in the population. Furthermore, the trend in divorce rates may again result in lone women caring, albeit often with the additional responsibility of children.

The social class of respondents was hard to assess. Twenty-eight certainly came from middle-class backgrounds and either had professional jobs, had married middle-class men, or had continued to live in their parents' middle-class home. Similarly, six were certainly working class. The remainder had for the most part experienced considerable social mobility through marriage or work, but in the case of single daughters were often still living at home and identified with their working-class backgrounds.[4]

Interviews and their interpretation

All respondents were interviewed for between one and four hours by one of the three interviewers – all of whom had extensive experience of interviewing elderly people – and the material was taped and transcribed. In developing the framework for the interviews, we drew on a range of interdisciplinary literature from oral history, social psychology, sociology, social policy, and the (largely feminist) literature on mother/daughter relationships.[5] The interviews were semi-structured and were designed to encourage respondents to reconstruct ther caring biographies, to comment on the central caring relationship and their relationships

4 The problems of assessing women's social class have provoked considerable controversy, see for example the exchange in *Sociology* 18 (November 1984).
5 Some of the material appears in the References section, but most of the background literature on conceptualizing the study appears in the Resource Bibliography.

with others, and to talk about their current self-image. Respondents were allowed to tell their stories without undue direction, although what they remembered, or the emphasis they accorded a particular issue, became integral to our interpretation of their experience. The way in which the interviews were conducted allowed respondents to mention telling details in the form of an aside, sometimes returning to the same example later on in the interview.

Of course, we recorded only the daughter's view of the matrix of relationships which comprise the caring experience. While it is important that these be understood as a necessary preliminary to effectively supporting the carer, in analysing the interviews we often had to exercise what in the end could only be our subjective judgement in drawing out of the narratives the way in which other participants contributed. For example, in considering the role of kin or support workers, we were often told that relatives or others had not contributed very significantly to caring, yet during the substance of the interview it would become evident that some support had been given. In some cases, the daughter appeared not to have recognized the mother's own perception of her situation – her own hopes and, more commonly, fears. In these instances, we made the decision to allow our interpretation to override the direct response of the daughter. The double subjectivity of such a study as this – that of the respondent and that of the researcher – is inevitable.

Another problem of interpretation arose when we considered the development of the caring relationship between mother and daughter, and the immediate and subsequent effect on the daughter's life. In several instances, we were told by the daughter that, for instance, she had given up work, or not advanced in her career as far as she might have hoped, because of her responsibilities for her mother. Other respondents reflected on the fact that they had not married or had children. In such cases it is difficult to draw a simple cause and effect conclusion; whereas the caring undoubtedly affected these aspects of the daughters' lives, whether it was the sole contributing factor is much harder to determine.

One of the most difficult issues in interpreting the interview material was the possibility of *ex post facto* rationalization. A few of our respondents had given considerable thought to their experiences and we had to judge the extent to which they had reinterpreted them. In other cases respondents told the interviewer that this was the first time they had either discussed or thought through their experiences as carers. While those responding directly to advertisements and letters tended to fall in the first category, careful examination of the data showed that the pattern of their experiences, particularly in respect to what we defined as problematic or supportive mother/daughter relationships, did not differ significantly from that of those who came to us by indirect referral. In other words as far as we can tell, respondents did not seek us out because they were anxious to tell a particularly negative or positive story.

The danger of 'prepared' responses, and of selectivity in memory were, we felt, minimized by the semi-structured nature and length of the interviews. Although respondents had clearly given consideration in advance to their caring tasks, they were less well prepared for our probing on caring relationships and the responses of others in the caring matrix. During wide-ranging interviews, the same topic was likely to arise in a number of ways and with a developing overall pattern. It was this wide-ranging discussion and approach to topics from different angles that in the end enabled the interviewers to feel that they could construct a valid 'caring biography' which described as accurately as possible the evolution of the caring experience.[6]

We were also aware that our respondents largely represented a particular age cohort which had grown to maturity during the war, and that we would have to balance the cohort effects against the cumulative effect of individual biographies (Hareven and Adams 1982; Plummer 1983; Bengston *et al.* 1985). Many of the single women in particular referred to 'my generation', conveying a sense of shared experience in respect to the war, particularly in respect to the loss of loved ones (often with veiled references to boyfriends and fiancés). Some also shared both a certain stigma attached to remaining unmarried, particularly in their mothers' eyes and what they perceived as their greater sense of obligation to parents than that of later generations. We were able additionally to reconstruct from their accounts the striking degree to which parents expected an unmarried daughter of this generation to live at home and the difficulty of doing otherwise when, for example, mortgage companies were reluctant to lend to single

6 Johnson (1978) has also advocated the use of biographies.

women. The range of choices of this cohort of women was considerably more circumscribed than would be the case today, and in particular the opportunity for autonomous living was small. This has implications not so much for the degree of affection or obligation towards parents, but for the nature of the women's expectations.

Use of interviews

The interviews covered issues of help and support for carers (financial, emotional, and practical): roles of 'others', including family, workmates, neighbours, and friends; and changing relationships between mothers and daughters, including historical references to the mother's own past in terms of work, family, and expectations for her daughter. The full range of these topics can be seen in the Interview Schedule reproduced in Appendix A.

During the course of the interview period, the researchers met frequently to discuss emerging themes and to consider how the great wealth of material could be used constructively. Two issues became evident very early on. First, similar terms and phrases were used unprompted by many carers: for example, what we called 'triggers' – stimuli which changed the focus of care – were common to many; and reactions to responses of kin and professionals were expressed in similar ways, as were self-perceptions. Second, at the same time, the interviewers themselves were developing insights into the changes in what we came to call the 'caring sequence'. Certain phrases became useful to describe how caring had started: 'drift', 'natural', or 'conscious choice'. Outcomes and responses fell into patterns to which we attached labels. It became evident that what was needed for the analysis of 'caring biographies' was a 'caring vocabulary', and to this we devoted considerable attention so that we were clear what each of us meant when using particular phrases or terms. This vocabulary is described in Appendix B, and we feel it contributes considerably to enabling a more sympathetic and precise description and assessment of the caring process.

Themes and ideas about the caring experience were analysed in two ways. A spread sheet was constructed so that coded information in respect to, for example, relationships, changes over time, mental and physical state of mother, helpfulness of kin and support workers, and responses of carers, could be displayed and useful comparisons made. In addition, for each respondent a graphic date chart was constructed, showing how work, caring, parents' and carers' life histories overlapped and interweaved. This enabled visual analysis of the effects on daughters and mothers of such events as the father's death or the mother suffering a sudden stroke. It was through these 'lines' that we became aware of the existence of different stages during the period of caring (see the discussion in chapter 3).

The emergence from the caring biographies of the pattern of contributory factors which constitute the caring experience has determined the overall structure of the book. It focuses in turn on the nature of the caring sequence, the central caring relationship, the carer's other relationships, and outside help. Thus quotations from interviews have had to some extent to be taken out of context in order to make comparisons within a thematic structure. We have tried to do this with care and without distorting the meaning of an isolated statement. The three case studies described in chapter 7 allow the interviews to be re-integrated to illustrate how certain contributory factors led to certain outcomes.

Abrams has written about the problems of finding a way of proceeding from soft data to hard evaluations in respect of investigations into social care (Abrams 1984). He identified the major difficulty as the way in which the distinctive forms of social care are 'embedded in relationships which in the language of Parsons, have to be seen as diffuse, particularistic, affective and ascriptive'. The task as Abrams defined it then became one of finding a way around the 'intractable informality' of social care in order to 'reduce informal caring relationships to the sort of units, factors, events, variables, items needed if specifiable inputs are to be systematically related to specifiable outcomes'. Abrams' concern to produce viable experimental approaches to the provision of informal care is admirable; however, we would suggest that the success of the kind of experimental research he had in mind – for example in the provision of good neighbour schemes – will nevertheless depend in large part on how informal caring relationships are conceptualized.

We would be the first to agree that there is no uniformity in the specifics of these, but just as recent work has succeeded in clarifying the nature and meaning of caring within the context of women's work and patterns of socialization, so it seemed to us that there was a place for an attempt to investigate empirically the nature of caring relationships and changes in them over time. We wanted to identify elements in the caring process as a way of constructing a meaningful framework within which to understand the nature and determinants of the interaction between carer and person cared for, and the relationships of carer and person cared for with significant others and with professional helpers. Many studies of carers attempt to assess the carer's needs at a particular point in time, often from a particular disciplinary perspective. Furthermore the relationship between helper and carer is assumed to be a linear one; however our research suggests that the reality of caring encompasses a complex web of relationships that must be understood before intervention can be effective.

Thus this study focuses on exploring the matrix of relationships that is caring and how they change over time. In so doing it is not our intention to 'problematize' caring. Our findings support the view that women *want* to care. However, they also show the central caring relationship between, in the case of this study, mothers and daughters, to be extremely intense and often difficult for a variety of reasons, ranging from the nature of the particular mother/daughter relationship to the practical problems and unpredictability of the caring task. We would suggest additionally that it is difficult for carers of the elderly to acknowledge their problems given the widespread fear of illness and death in our society and the resulting taboos of talking about these issues. Because the study focuses on daughters as carers and is complicated by the special qualities pertaining to the mother/daughter relationship, and because it focuses on the experience of co-resident care, the extent to which its findings may be generalizable to all carers and to other caring situations remains to be established by further research.

CHAPTER 2

Why care?

A 'DECISION' TO CARE?

We set out to determine how women reached the decision to care, but it transpired that only ten made the decision consciously. The rest either 'drifted' into caring, usually because they were already living with their mothers, or were unable to relate to the idea of consciously considering whether to care. For them, caring for their mothers was above all a 'natural' stage in the life course.

It has already been suggested that any explanation of women's willingness to care requires consideration of the female psyche, the workings of family relationships, particularly in respect to feelings of affection and obligation, and women's material circumstances. Our semi-structured interviews were capable only of eliciting feelings, attitudes, and perceptions. We had no means of assessing the importance of personality, but five respondents indicated that caring met a definite need of their own to be involved in looking after others, to feel loved and wanted. One woman who cared for both her parents said: 'To feel wanted and that's the most important part . . . To feel wanted. I tell you when I felt most discontent was when they were having a good spell.' The suggestion that caring is fundamentally a part of the female identity is also born out in the notion of caring as 'natural', clearly expressed by nine of our respondents. This provides some support for the idea that women's willingness to care may stem from a concern for others that is central to the development of femininity. As one married respondent put it: 'You find it quite impossible to walk away from doing it.' Such feelings seem to run deeper than ties of affection and obligation, strong as these may also be, and were as likely to characterize the responses of married as single respondents.

In many respects, the idea that a child should separate from its parents and move away, which Litwak (1985) and Willmott (1986) have described as characterizing 'the modified extended family', was poorly developed in the vast majority of our respondents. Nor could it be said that relationships between these mothers and daughters provided confirmation for Hess and Waring's (1978) view that relations between parents and children in later life lack clear normative prescriptions. In the words of one respondent, looking after mother was something she naturally 'grew into'.

For the most part, our respondents did not expect to separate fully from their parents. In large part their behaviour was structured or at the very least reinforced by their material circumstances, which are in turn closely related to the experiences of this particular group of women. Single women who reached maturity around the period of the war usually expected and were expected by their parents to live at home; twenty of the single respondents and one married respondent had always lived at home other than for brief periods of wartime service. A college-educated respondent whose mother was also a professional woman, found it quite natural to return to live at home in the 1950s after she had been widowed. She pointed out that not only was this socially acceptable, but it was also cheaper: 'It just seemed natural that a daughter should come home, and live a great deal more cheaply after all.' Several respondents made this point. In the days before mortgages were commonly granted to single women, living at home was often the more comfortable option: 'I hadn't much money in those days. . . . To get a home of my own I'd have had to have gone into digs and I'd have had to take my dog.' The married respondent who had always lived with her mother had done so because accommodation was in such short supply after the war.

It also seems that parents and respondents' peer groups expected that single daughters would both live at home and care for their mothers. One explained that her parents did not expect her to leave home other than to get married and to have done so would have been experienced by them as a rejection. The attitudes of parents were often conflicting. Several respondents reported feeling that their mothers both wanted them to get married and also to stay at home to provide help and companionship. Anthea Ducquenin's (1984) oral history of single women growing up around the First World War has documented situations in which the marriage opportunities of a daughter were sometimes deliberately foiled by parents in order to keep her at home. Such deliberate manipulation was not reported by our respondents, but parental ambivalence was clear: 'I think she would have liked me to get married because it would show her daughter was the same as everyone else. It was quite the thing . . . but she would also like her daughter to be with her.' Here the stigma attached to spinsterhood clearly conflicted with the mother's desire for her daughter's company.

Friends and neighbours as well as parents added to the expectation that a single daughter would care. One respondent's friends were also all single women and also all cared for their mothers. Thus her circle expected her to care, but also provided her with support. Another respondent who had experienced strong support from neighbours while caring also spoke of the case of one elderly neighbour whose daughter lived nearby but showed no sign of taking her in: 'I'd be ashamed . . . it's a disgrace. We all think in the road it's a disgrace.' Inevitably, women who always lived with their mothers 'drifted' into caring for them, whereas those who had moved away from home to work or to marry were usually faced with a conscious decision about caring. However, in nine cases, the decision to move back home or invite mother to live with them was made while the mother was still well and mobile. These decisions may therefore be linked to a deep-seated concern for others and to the idea of caring as a broadly based sense of connection. These women felt that their mothers should not have to live alone and thereafter drifted into caring as their mothers' health deteriorated. In retrospect, two of these respondents felt that they had thereby allowed their mothers to get too dependent on them too early: 'You can lead them into a situation where they become a lot more dependent on you . . . had I not been available to my parents . . . I think they would have been a lot more independent.' Thirteen invited their mothers to live with them, or themselves moved home, only when the mother also required care; in seven cases this coincided with the death of the respondent's father.

WHY YOU?

Those taking a conscious decision to live with or to care for their mothers were also subject to particular circumstances that prompted their action. A conscious decision about caring was far more likely to occur when there were other siblings who might have cared, a brother, or more controversially still, a sister. Only daughters were more likely to consider living together and caring as 'natural', or to drift into it. Siblings are often regarded in the abstract as additional pools of caring support. However, our data provided considerable evidence of fierce sibling rivalry and bitterness. In contrast, only one respondent expressed bitterness at being an only child. Three of the twenty only daughters expressed the unsolicited view that while they had initially wished they had someone else with whom to share the burden of caring, they now felt that perhaps the arguments over who was to do what would have been too great: 'The care falls on one, on the other hand I don't have the thought that brother Fred or sister Joan aren't doing their share. I had no option, but that makes it easier in some ways', and: 'I used to think it was a bad thing, I wished I had brothers and sisters, but since then I've thought it was better, I hear a lot of them arguing over who doesn't want whom . . . if you're the only one you make the decisions.'

Eleven respondents had brothers, but none were reported to have played a particularly active part in supporting the carer. Three carers felt no resentment about this; one, with a strong sense of appropriate sex roles, felt it would have been quite unnatural for her brothers to care: 'My brothers couldn't wash her and dress her and wash her hair could they? . . . I was the daughter, I would do it, yes.' On the other hand three were bitter: 'I feel it's all wrong that the single one in the family should be the one that does everything. At one stage I told him [the brother] that lots of single daughters dropped dead looking after their mother. He just got in his car and drove off . . . he was a fine sort of brother really.' In four cases the respondent felt that her brother's wife was responsible for his refusal to share the care, for example: 'His wife said, "I'm having nothing to do with her" – I knew where I stood. Full stop . . . She couldn't stand illness . . . from the outset I knew there would be no help from my brother.'

For the most part sisters seem to have played a more active role than brothers. Two pairs of unmarried sisters lived together and shared the care of their mother. One respondent whose sister lived abroad nevertheless insisted that this sister also shared the care because she would fly in at a moment's notice and would take their mother for extended holidays. Another, with a married sister in the same village, felt that she had done all she could, given her large family. Two appear to have been resentful that a married sister did not do more, but more general was a feeling of injustice that a single daughter should always be considered to be the obvious carer. Four felt that the work of the single daughter caring for an elderly parent went largely unrecognized, while mothers caring for children got considerably more help and sympathy:

> Really it was for the single women in those days and I still think the single women need more help than the married. The married have got a husband earning their living. We've still got to earn a living and run the home and do everything. I mean if they've got a home and children they can sometimes do little jobs, do an errand or shopping. I had to do all this myself.

Nevertheless three respondents also said that they felt that to have combined marriage and caring would have been quite impossible. One was engaged for an extended period and in the end her fiancé died before her mother. The conflict between different kinds of caring, all of which may be considered 'natural' by and for women, is something to which we shall return.

Those who accepted caring as 'natural' never questioned what had happened. However, those drifting into or consciously deciding to care believed firmly in retrospect (not necessarily with bitterness) that they had had little alternative but to care, both because of their own and/or their mothers' objections to institutional care, and because of either the unavailability of others to care or the unwillingness of siblings to assume the responsibility. The question of who else might have cared confirms the idea of the existence of a caring hierarchy in which the daughter is the first choice and, we would suggest, a single daughter is preferred to a married daughter.

The autonomy of single women has increased dramatically in recent decades, yet it is unlikely that the existence of this caring hierarchy has been significantly modified. One respondent indicated implicitly that she thought it had not when she said: 'The role of women has changed so much hasn't it? I don't really see why it should fall on the woman honestly.' It is also clear that when a daughter drifts into, or decides to care, she shoulders the whole responsibility. The position is analogous to women's continued responsibility for housework: husbands may help, but the wife still has the responsibility not only for the brunt of the work but deciding what and how it should be done. Commenting on the lack of help she received from relatives one respondent said: 'It's usually left to one person.' Resentment about this arises not so much from the task of caring itself, an obligation which the majority of our respondents welcomed, but as Carole Pateman (1979) has observed in another context, from the fact that the duty to care is imposed as a result of their position as single women in the caring hierarchy. In this respect it is not chosen and may impede other goals including other desires to care, especially for husbands and children.

The tensions experienced in respect to the role of other siblings in providing care demonstrate for the most part clear acceptance of traditional sex roles. Where there was bitterness about brothers it was more likely to arise from an apparent lack of recognition of the work of the carer and the neglect of the sort of duties that were considered to be appropriate, for example visiting regularly and facilitating breaks either by paying for them, arranging them, or providing respite care. Brothers were not on the whole expected to share the responsibility for care. In their attitudes towards sisters, especially married sisters, respondents revealed conflicting emotions: resentment that caring for children received more recognition than caring for the elderly, and a feeling that married women got a better deal generally.

These feelings all relate to the way in which women are motivated to care throughout the life course for husbands, children, and dependent relatives; and the conflicts they experience in fulfilling their caring obligations. Our single women respondents were correct in their observations that marriage meant such conflicts had to be dealt with on a daily basis, but as members of a generation for whom spinsterhood carried particular opprobrium, they nevertheless regretted the absence of other caring responsibilities for husbands and children. In some cases caring for an elderly mother undoubtedly substituted for other forms of caring: 'You're bound to think sometimes what your life might have been. And when your sister brings in new babies and that. I would admit, my maternal instinct was turned into them, and they became my children, but I knew they weren't my children and I would get told off every now and again.' As will be shown later, in some cases such feelings may lead the carer to guard jealously her caring role against intrusion.

AFFECTION OR OBLIGATION?

Those taking a conscious decision to care were additionally more subject to the pull between ties of affection and/or duty and other personal considerations. Those who had moved away from home were more likely to have had expectations that depended on greater autonomy. A respondent who gave up college to return home to care for her mother had always intended to go back, but twenty-two years of caring made this impossible. Feelings of obligation and affection were universal in our sample, but the balance between these differed enormously. Those for whom caring appeared above all as a natural task were more likely to express strong affection for their mothers: 'Love took me through this.' It is almost impossible to say whether there were many cases in which affection was entirely absent, although in eight cases very little was expressed: 'We weren't particularly close, we got on all right, and I was really the dutiful daughter . . . I mean not grudgingly, but I mean we weren't that close really, no.' The study by Levin, Sinclair, and Gorbach (1983) of the supporters of the confused elderly found that six in ten mentioned the tie of kinship and one in four love when speaking of the reasons for caring, and that those who had lived with the elderly person for a long time (which was the case with almost half our respondents) were more likely to give love as the motivating factor.

Blau (1973) has suggested that close bonds of affection and intimacy between parents and children will not last long because modern society emphasizes independence between the generations. This was not true of the respondents in this study, most of whom in any case exhibited relatively little expectation or desire for autonomy. Blau's hypothesis may prove more true when applied to the behaviour of present and future generations, although it is unlikely that cause and effect will be so clear cut. Nor does it seem to be a simple matter, as Hess and Waring (1983) have suggested, of a shift in intergenerational relations from the obligatory to the voluntary, resulting in a conflict in expectations between the elderly person and the potential caregiver. Given that the injunction to care is a more complex matter than can be explained by either ties of affection or obligation, there is likely to be a conflict between an enduring desire to care and increasing female autonomy and expectations of equal opportunities (Brody *et al.* 1983).

Most of our respondents held feelings of affection and obligation in a delicate balance and talked about them as sides of the same coin: 'I think you've got to think a great deal of somebody or have a great sense of duty to be able to do it. [Which?] Some of each. I think I thought that it was mostly duty . . . there are times when you hate each other when you are in a relationship like that.' Indeed affection shades imperceptibly into duty with the phrase 'it's your mother', when it is uttered with a shrug rather than in a tone of something that is patently self-evident. Attempts such as that of Bengston and Troll (1978) to measure 'sentiment' as opposed to 'solidary attachment' pose major difficulties, and like the attempt to abstract the labour of 'tending' from the labour and love of caring mean that the essential ambivalence experienced by carers is disregarded.

The idea of there being an obligation or duty to care was frequently referred to by respondents, but the most common expression, 'well, it's your mum', covered a variety of ideas, ranging from that of paying back a debt, to a desire to protect or indeed to please or seek the approval of the mother. Duty to a mother was more keenly felt than to a father, something Firth, Hubert, and Forge (1969) also observed in their study of middle-class family relationships. A majority of our respondents expressed some sense of repaying their mothers for past sacrifices on their behalf or simply for having cared for them as children: 'Well, I think really, if you can't look after your own mother when she gets . . . that's the way I look at it . . . I think you *should* – they looked after you didn't they? I may be old-fashioned, but there . . . '

A striking number of mothers (eleven) had been widowed while the respondents were still children, which increased feelings of obligation:

My mother only got 10/-, and 5/- for me [widow's pension] . . . she did some charring. . . . I obviously love her very much when I think of all she did for me then . . . she could have put me in an orphanage, but she didn't and I'm certainly not going to put her in an old people's home if she doesn't want it. [The tenses here are muddled. In fact the respondent's mother had just voluntarily entered a home about which the respondent felt very ambivalent.]

Several authors (Isaacs, Livingstone, and Neville 1972; Sheldon 1982; Fennel, Phillipson, and Wenger 1983) have suggested that the quality of the early relationship between parent and child is important for understanding later developments. This may give some indication as to the variation in the motives underlying the injunction to care. In two cases, one where the mother had been an alcoholic and another where she had given her daughter no support and disapproved of her marriage, the sense of obligation to care was still strong. In both these cases the respondents appeared still to be seeking their mothers' approval: 'I wanted to take her because I don't think anyone should be put in a home, unless it's necessary . . . it was very difficult . . . I was trying to please her.' Similar feelings were expressed by three other respondents whose relationships with their mothers were considerably less traumatic.

In his historical study of family relationships in Lancashire, Michael Anderson (1971) has argued that parent/child relations were a matter of careful calculation, old mothers were invited into their children's home because of the services they could provide in the way of babysitting, mending etc. But as Hareven (1982) has pointed out, this does not account for reciprocal relationships between the generations that do not operate on the basis of current exchange, but rather over an extended period of time. Several respondents reported that their mothers had made substantial sacrifices for them which they felt honour bound to repay by caring: 'I went to a central school because my Mum was very hard up, but somehow she found enough to buy a uniform for me. And I went to school till I was 16, which must have been hard for her, mustn't it?' Others spoke of their mothers working long hours and of their desire to be able to provide some comfort for them in their old age. One, whose mother worked in a butcher's shop until she was over 70 said: 'She worked such a long time. I wanted her to have a bit more on retirement.' In fourteen cases, the mother had herself cared for a husband or an elderly dependant – usually her mother or an aunt – and the respondents tended to feel that caring was 'a natural sort of thing in our family' and a tradition that should be continued.

Seven respondents felt very protective towards their mothers, often as a result of their mother's widowhood or because of bad relationships with fathers: 'She was a dear but she was – that's her golden wedding up there [pointing to a photograph] – she was a dear but she was so helpless.' Several were reluctant to leave their mothers to their fathers' doubtful care: 'If she'd have been left with my father he'd have had her in a home . . . she couldn't cope you see . . . the atmosphere was so awful and I thought of my mum going to be ill and she's going to have this all the time, my dad nagging about his tea not being ready . . . he would have led her a dog's life.' A respondent whose mother suffered from Alzheimer's Disease felt a strong desire to protect her from the censure of those who had no understanding of the disease: 'I always wanted to protect her. I always wanted to cover up the faults.' Only in a small minority of cases was there any evidence to suggest that feelings of obligation had been actively induced by the mother. In two cases the unmarried daughter had been given the parental home while the mother was still alive with the strong expectation, albeit implicit, that she would care in return.

On the whole, respondents talked more about ties of obligation based primarily on notions of reciprocity than they did about affection, although there is a sense in which for the vast majority the fulfilling of obligations was predicated on affection. Cicirelli (1983) may well be right in his suggestion that obligation works through attachment. To reach any firm conclusions about the degree to which women care for reasons to do with the development of their psyches, their material circumstances, or feelings of affection and obligation arising from kin relationships, would require a much larger study including in its sample women who had, despite it all, decided *not* to care. Women may feel that caring is 'natural', may 'drift' into it, or may make a conscious decision about it depending on the mix of psychological, emotional, and material factors involved. One thing is clear, the idea of caring as a simple act of altruism on the part of one family member out of love for another has little basis in reality. The vast majority of our sample felt that caring was the right thing to have done, whether out of a sense of duty, affection, a feeling that there was no alternative, or because it never crossed their minds to do otherwise.

Once the co-resident caring relationship is established it becomes central. The carer may be able to call on a variety of informal, voluntary and professional helpers, but she assumes final responsibility for caring and the person cared for is dependent on her. In the case of single daughters who had always lived with their mothers there was of course no sharp division between co-resident living and co-resident caring, the one often shaded into the other. Married daughters were more likely to find the nature of ther responsibilities sharply redefined, although further research may well reveal that a principal carer is clearly identified both by a network of supporters and by the elderly person while the latter is still living alone.

CHAPTER 3

The caring task

The collection of respondents' caring biographies revealed wide differences in the nature and length of their caring experiences. Our technique of developing 'caring biographies' enabled us to identify stages in what we have called the 'caring sequence'. These stages reflected both the physical and mental states of the mother, as well as the daughter's response to them. The caring period involved movement between these stages, usually from what we have identified as semi-care to either full care or part-time full care. (Appendix B provides an extended discussion of these and other terms.) However, not all respondents passed through all stages and it should not be assumed that there was necessarily a natural progression from one stage to the other.

The period of full care, defined as the period during which the mother required such personal tending as to make it impossible for the daughter to leave her for more than an hour or two other than with a substitute carer, varied from six weeks to twenty-two years, with a period of somewhere between two and five years being the most common. However, full care was usually preceded by periods of 'semi-care' and sometimes by 'part-time full care'. Semi-care is characterized by the carer's feeling that her mother should not be left alone for an extended period, especially overnight and in the evenings. Little or no personal tending is involved at this stage and the tie consists almost entirely of the carer's sense of responsibility for the mother. Sometimes this involved primarily surveillance, for instance to ensure that the mother had not fallen, and at other times was characterized more by the carer's sense of duty or loyalty, and the feeling that she was not able to go out and leave her mother on her own except for 'acceptable' reasons, such as going to work. We defined part-time full care as a period during which the mother's condition warranted 'full care', but the daughter managed to carry on looking after her family without becoming overwhelmed by caring for her mother, or carried on working, either by making arrangements for someone to come in or by trusting to luck that all would be well with her mother, always ensuring she was home by certain times each evening in order to get through the amount of work accruing from the care required by her mother, as well as for her own maintenance. It appears to us that the caring task is determined not only by the mother's state of physical and mental health, but also by both parties' perceptions of the situation as a whole.

THE CARING SEQUENCE

Not all respondents passed through all three stages of caring. Four respondents experienced extended periods of semi-care at a distance, undertaking co-resident care only when their mothers required full care. Others, who invited their mothers to live with them when they were still well, together with many unmarried women who had always lived with their mothers, were suddenly plunged into either part-time full or full care as a result of their mothers suffering a stroke or developing cancer, for example. The length of the period of semi-care and part-time full care is reflected in the variation of the age of the carers when care began. Studies show women carers to be typically women in their fifties. Given that our respondents had been caring within the last ten years, we would have expected the vast majority to be now in their fifties and sixties. Table 3.1 shows this indeed proved to be the case. However, there was a somewhat larger range of ages at which caring actually began.

Table 3.1   *Age distribution of carers*

	Age now	Age at commencement of full-time caring
10–19	–	1
20–29	–	3
30–39	–	6
40–49	5	8
50–59	9	18
60–69	21	5
70+	6	–

While respondents usually undertook full care in their 50s and 60s, this was often preceded by varying periods of semi-care and part-time full care. It should also be noted that in very occasional cases, the caring sequence was not progressive, and a period of full care – during a serious illness, for example – might be succeeded by another, sometimes lengthy, period of part-time full care or even semi-care. Our definition of semi-care encompasses the kind of tie the carer feels when the mother is admitted to a hospital or nursing home.

It is not always easy to mark the passage from one stage in the caring sequence to another, both because of problems of memory and because most respondents stressed that the change was gradual. This was particularly true of the shift from semi-care to part-time full care and of cases in which the mother was a victim of senile dementia. On the other hand, it was sometimes possible to identify a number of 'triggers' that signalled a deterioration in the mother's condition and an increased burden of care for the daughter. Many writers (Wenger 1984; Willmott 1986) have reported widowhood as the occasion for the beginning of a period of co-resident care. Of the twenty respondents who experienced a period of geographical separation from their mothers, six resumed living with them at this point and eight of the sample as a whole dated the period of their mother's deterioration in health from the date of their father's death. As one woman whose mother suffered depression after her father's death put it: 'She shut herself away, you see, she was like Queen Victoria after my father died.' Another reported: 'After that mum let me take over, she didn't want to know, she lost the will a bit.' In this case, as in two others, the mother had nursed the father through a prolonged illness. One woman reported that her father had died from bowel cancer and her mother had nursed him until his death: 'She was marvellous – wonderful – they had been married 60 years that week [of his death]. I think that really, slowly, she went downhill after that.'

Turning points in the mother's health were also triggered by other events removed from the mother herself. In one case the mother seemed to keep going until her daughter retired from work:

That summer she said, 'Oh, I'm dreading you going back to school' . . . but um . . . at the Christmas I retired and whether at that point she thought, you know, 'Oh, I'm all right' now that she'd got me at home I don't know, but um she did seem to be more . . . dependent from the time I stayed at home . . . I suppose she was trying to keep herself going before that.

Another woman dated her mother's increased need for care from her brother's wedding, after which her Alzheimer's Disease worsened significantly.

Widowhood often inaugurated a period of semi-care. Initially it was not unusual for the mother's dependence to be as much or more psychological as physical. Several respondents described their mothers as having been totally dependent on their husbands in respect to anything concerning the world outside the home and this dependency was transferred to the daughter. One respondent described her mother's dependency rather contemptuously:

She was a typical Victorian housewife. They always wanted some bolstering up and usually it was their husband. She relied on him utterly, I could never rely on anyone like that. She did her job here [at home] but that's as far as her mind went. She was a timid person. She would give us hell in here but wouldn't say boo to a goose outside.

When her father died her mother 'expected me to take up the reins. She never ever took any responsibility.' Helen Evers' (1983, 1984, 1985) research into the experiences of elderly women living alone found two broad responses to everyday life, that of the 'active initiator', who feels herself to be in charge of her life, and that of the 'passive responder', who appears to lack positive control over her existence. The former seem to be distinguished by the fact that they had worked outside the home, while the latter had spent their lives caring for others. A majority of our respondents' mothers would appear to fit Evers' 'passive respondent' category. As one aim of our study was to ascertain carers' preferences for their own future care needs, it was tempting to try to apply Evers' concept to our carers as well as to their mothers. However, some caution must be exercised in extending the use of such a typology to those caring for elderly people. For, as we shall see, many of our respondents developed skills in dealing with professional service providers as a result of caring that are unlikely to render them passive responders in their turn, even though much of their lives has been spent in caring for others.

THE BEGINNING OF CARE

When respondents began to care, it was usually with little or no sense of how long or how difficult and intense a commitment it would prove to be. This was obviously most characteristic of those who 'drifted' into caring, but those taking a conscious decision to invite their mothers to live with them often did not think that they would become dependent so soon, and those consciously deciding to care had no idea how long the caring period would prove to be. One respondent who had lived in warm companionship with her active, independent mother all her life described the profound readjustment that was necessary when her mother had a stroke at age 91, which almost immediately immobilized her and made her incontinent:

> She dozed off. Then she woke up and she went to get up and she couldn't. It happened as easily and as quickly as that. I thought her knee had given way. I got her upstairs – it was very difficult. The next morning she voiced it and I thought it: 'I think I've had a little stroke'.
>
> [Her mother went into hospital for about ten days.] I said, couldn't she come home. He [the doctor] said 'Why, is she getting agitated?' I said, 'Oh, no, I want her back home.' But he kept her in a few more days. I think it was for my sake as much as anything. It was quite strange to be at home – I mean I went to the hospital twice a day so I wasn't that free – but I did have a week. I did go to town one day.
>
> At the beginning I always thought that when someone her age had a stroke, another one would follow, perhaps, and it would prove more or less fatal. I'd always hoped she would go quickly when her time came, but of course it wasn't to be, it wasn't to be at all. [The respondent had just retired.] When you've been sitting all these hours in an office, it took me a long while – I used to get very, very tired. The balls of my feet used to ache. My skirts used to slide round me . . .
>
> She didn't sleep too well the first year – she would ask for a cup of tea at night and I would give it to her, and she would say, 'You have a cup of tea', and I'd say, 'Mother, I don't want a cup of tea. I want to go to bed.'

In comparing their lot with that of married women looking after children, several respondents made the point that the period of child dependency was finite, whereas there was no knowing how long the period of caring for an elderly dependant would last. Phillipson (1982) has commented on the strain that longevity placed on informal carers and his observation that carers sometimes think 'she might go on forever' was certainly reflected in the comments of our respondents, ten of whom referred to the difficulty of coping with the idea of 'great tracts of time' passing. Three said they coped by taking one day at a time: 'I consciously decided it was no good moaning and groaning because I couldn't do this or that, so I decided to take one day at a time and be an opportunist.' The degree of difficulty experienced by carers in dealing with the uncertainty of the caring sequence depended in part on the nature of the mother's condition – those whose mothers developed cancer, for example, felt that the nature of their commitment had a considerably more finite quality than those who cared for mothers with a chronic condition, such as arthritis – and in part on the daughter's own circumstances.

Of particular importance was the point at which caring took place in relation to the daughter's stage in the life course and her expectations. If the burden of caring became heavy when the daughter was still in middle age, then it was often particularly difficult for her to decide whether to give up work, for example, and sacrifice pension entitlements. Two sisters who cared for their mother and found themselves facing this dilemma put it like this:

> You see you didn't know if you said somebody will be ill for so long, you could get time off or ask for leave without pay and then go back, or something like that, but we didn't know how – nobody could tell us whether this was just going to go on for *years* or whether it was just . . . so it was very difficult to make a decision on what to do for the best.

In this case, one sister had just decided that she would have to retire prematurely when the mother died. In such circumstances the carer may well shoulder a very heavy burden of what we have termed part-time full care both for financial reasons and in order to keep a fulfilling job.

Carers whose mothers' needs for care increase substantially when they themselves are in their late fifties may well opt for early retirement. Eleven of our respondents took this course. Several others reduced their workload, followed less demanding career paths, or had already left or reduced their work because of their father's ill health. Like all other patterns we traced, cause and effect were not always easy to establish, caring being only one of several factors involved. One married women respondent who fully expected and wished to look after her mother at some point had thought that the need to do so would not arise until some ten years later than proved to be the case. Robinson and Thurnher (1979) have noted that the coincidence of a parent's demands and a child's awareness of a shrinking future may well cause stress. This respondent and her husband had made careful plans for themselves, taking out a mortgage on the basis of two incomes, and had calculated that the respondent might have to take time out in her fifties (her current age) to care:

> If the whole thing had happened now, which is perhaps the time I thought maybe it might have happened, our whole financial position would have been different, and I think this happens to a lot of people. You think these things are always going to happen in a nice order, it's all going to happen when we've got – yet it doesn't of course, and this is the problem. If it hits you at the wrong time because you've already committed your money in other ways . . . sensible planning can let you down.

Our working-class respondents tended to have less firm life-course expectations and to experience less tension in this respect. Both Nissel and Bonnerjea (1982) and Marsden and Abrams (1987) observed (on the basis of larger working-class samples than we obtained) that middle-class carers seemed to experience more stress. We would suggest that if this is borne out by future investigations, it may be related to their different (and greater) expectations in respect to daily routines, social proprieties, and social contacts.

THE ACCUMULATION OF CARING RESPONSIBILITIES

The semi-care tie usually required more of the daughter than filling-in for father. One respondent moved in with both her parents in the early 1950s. Her father died in 1974 and her mother in 1984, aged 94. The daughter very gradually became more concerned about, and more responsible in an indefinable way, for her mother. The period of full care was a matter of only six weeks immediately prior to the mother's death. When the respondent was asked when she felt the additional weight of responsibility, she was unable to answer, but prompting elicited that while she did not feel it at her father's death, she certainly did five years after that. By this time she was taking her mother's needs more and more into consideration whenever making her own plans. This period of hard-to-define dependency is characterized by respondents saying things like: 'Well, I had to take her wishes into account'; 'She didn't like it when I/we went away on holiday'; 'I felt I couldn't go out at night because she would be on her own'; and 'Of course I couldn't take a job that involved more travel.' These constraints arose from the mother's expressed and implied needs and the perceptions of the daughter.

Periods of semi-care develop their own routines. One woman's mother had a stroke in 1964 after which she was practically paralysed down one side:

> She did not have the full use of the hand or leg, but she could walk around and she managed to dress herself – I let her do it because I'd got a full-time job. I used to cook her meals, precook them, and she just had to turn the gas on. We could go away on holiday, staying in suitable hotels. We went on that way very well really until 1976 [at which point her mother had another heart attack and a bad fall which entailed full care by the daughter].

In cases where care of this sort persisted for much longer periods, perhaps with little co-operation on the part of the mother and few breaks for the daughter, the strain was considerable. Another respondent had little or no personal tending to do, but her mother's condition made her liable to fall. This woman had thirty-three years during which she always felt responsible for her mother and during which her mother exerted pressure on her to be at home.

Semi-care often shades into part-time full care, when the mother becomes increasingly dependent, but the respondent continues to go out to work. A respondent who undertook seven years of part-time full care after her mother suffered a stroke that left her housebound, talked of the routine she had to follow:

> [In the morning] I had to get her up and set her up for the day

and hope she'd be all right. [In the evening] I bathed her – she loved to have a bath. . . . I did the veggies for the next day and cut the sandwiches the night before, usually it was half past eight or twenty to nine before I sat down and then she'd say, 'Oh, aren't you going to come and talk to me?'

Another experienced eleven years of part-time full care during the last five years of which her mother, who had multiple sclerosis, became severely disabled. Before this her mother needed a lot of attention which was provided on an *ad hoc* basis by nurses and home helps:

It was the time in between when she wasn't terribly badly disabled when I felt most trapped, was most trapped. [In what way?] Because she couldn't – you know – she couldn't look after – she couldn't get up, she couldn't go to bed on her own, you know there was 24 hours in the day that she couldn't be left entirely – I never gave up my job.

It was only after this respondent collapsed that more systematic help was provided – hence she felt less 'trapped' during the last five years when her mother's disability was, in fact, worse.

Periods of semi-care are often distinguished by the lack of any professional help from outside. While the primary caring relationship usually intensifies during periods of full care, the carer's burden may be substantially eased by increased recognition of her need for help. Nine of our respondents felt bitter that they had been allowed to reach, or come near to, breaking point before help was forthcoming.

A recent study (Jones, Victor, and Vetter 1983) of 657 elderly people and their carers, showed that 66 per cent of the main helpers experienced some effect on their own health. Nine of our respondents experienced a breakdown before or after co-resident care ended, but a further twenty-two mentioned some health problem related to caring. Two women mentioned the difficulties they encountered being menopausal during the period of full-time care. Back trouble and the strain of lifting were also commonly mentioned, but the most frequent complaint was of physical and mental exhaustion:

You go *years*. I never knew what it was to have a whole night's sleep. You're just on the edge of sleep all the time. And in the last year I used to fall into bed thinking it's only eight hours or seven hours till I have to start the whole thing again, you know.

Setting the alarm clock at regular (sometimes two-hourly) intervals, or becoming a very light sleeper were commonly reported. A respondent who enjoyed a very companionable relationship with her mother nevertheless experienced difficulty in this respect. Her mother developed the habit of getting up countless times in the night. 'I would say, "Please go back to bed, I am so tired", and she would say. "Why should I go to bed because you are tired?" There was no answer to that [laugh].' This respondent developed a system whereby she placed her bed so that she could see through the open door to her mother's bed and thereby assess whether her mother needed assistance without getting up. Four respondents shared a bedroom with their mothers; several moved their mothers downstairs; and six others either moved mothers in with grandchildren, or themselves slept in the living room of a one-bedroomed flat. Such arrangements served to increase the intensity of the relationship and in many cases contributed to lack of privacy and stress for the carer and/or the rest of the family. Some sense of territoriality was in fact a crucial part of those mother/ daughter relationships that seem to have worked best (see Chapter 4).

The build-up of stress as a result of these sorts of circumstances can be imperceptible:

I don't think you're aware [of stress] when you go through it. You know you're upset, but you're too busy thinking what's going to happen next. I used to say I didn't have time to be ill. I've also realized that you shouldn't drive when you're like this, but then what do you do? I had two bumps.

This respondent, like many others, lost a considerable amount of weight. Another was told by her doctor that she should let him know when she could no longer cope. After this she started to keep a diary because as she tellingly remarked: 'It's very difficult to know when you can't cope.' This was confirmed by another similar comment: 'You have to think of yourself as well. There's no reason why you should be killed by having more than human beings can stand . . . it's very hard to stand outside yourself and say, "I also matter here. I can't do it." ' One of the greatest fears of carers seems to be that they will 'crack up' and won't be able to 'see it through'.

Two respondents raised the sensitive issue of violence, albeit at one remove from themselves: 'I can understand people who resort to suffocating a parent, particularly if they're suffering a lot and the carer is feeling very tired, because people give you a lot of stupid advice, but they won't give you any practical help.' And: 'You hear a lot about granny-bashing and you think, "Oh rubbish", then you realize how easy it is because you get to the state you're trying to keep your self control and it's gradually going and you know if you're not careful it'll go.' This woman experienced only a year's full-time caring and virtually no semi-care or part-time full care, demonstrating that susceptibility to the stress arising from caring varies enormously.

DEALING WITH THE CARING TASKS

The tolerance for undertaking different types of caring tasks is also subject to wide variation. Nineteen mothers experienced only physical illness, eleven mental illness only; a further eleven were both physically and mentally ill at the end of the caring period. Some respondents felt particular antipathy towards tasks of personal tending, others were more upset by the process of mental deterioration. One appeared to contradict herself on this: 'I have always said I'd rather deal with a mental thing than a physical thing because I don't like having to deal with commodes and what have you'; later in the interview, she said: 'I could have faced the physical things if it hadn't been for the mental side. If she'd been a different person who would accept in a cheerful way, have a joke about it, but no, she couldn't do that.' In effect, this respondent disliked physical tending and also found her mother's increasing senility and contrariness very wearying. Another woman spoke tolerantly of her mother's mental confusion as something she could not help, but felt embarrassed and revolted by her incontinence. Respondents often commented to the effect that it would be worse if they had to cope with mental illness as well as physical incapacity or vice versa. Two stated firmly that the demented elderly were better off in an institution because the strain of watching a loved one deteriorate in this way was too great: 'In *my* case the emotional tie was a *good* thing, but if it's somebody who's senile, it's a very bad thing.'

The strain of coping with personality change in the confused elderly is well documented (Isaacs, Livingstone, and Neville

1972; Levin, Sinclair and Gorbach 1983). Six per cent of people over 65 and 22 per cent of the over-80s are likely to become confused. Levin, Sinclair, and Gorbach identified four dimensions to the problems of supporters of the confused elderly: behavioural, interpersonal, practical, and social. The last three are also common to supporters of the physically incapable, although some of the major practical problems posed by physical incapacity, for example, propensity to fall and incontinence, tend also to accompany dementia, thus compounding the burden of carers for the confused. Behavioural problems and the deterioration of a close kin relationship are more likely to be the special province of carers of the confused elderly:

> With Alzheimer's, see, you've got to think . . . here's your knife, here's your fork, eat your dinner, you know. I was literally her brain for her . . . put on the light for them, tell them to sit down on the toilet, tell them to stand up, pull up their knicks, come over to the sink, give me your teeth, here's your mouth wash, here's the soap, rinse your hands . . . well, if you're doing that for a year twice a day, you know . . .

The resigned manner and dull monotonous tone in which this was said captured the daily grind of getting the mother to do every little thing.

Mothers who wandered, accused a grandchild of stealing, made 'puddings' with Vim and washing-up liquid, or who resisted their carer's best efforts to help or assist, provided a catalogue of misery and strain. Confusion was always accompanied by a decreasing ability to communicate and often by a tendency to physical aggression. Respondents found the former distressing for practical and emotional reasons:

> She couldn't really carry on a conversation . . . when she was trying to talk to you you didn't really know what she was saying [laughs], so it was quite frustrating really. . . . [We communicated] only by a sort of guesswork, suggesting to her what she might want to do you know, which made it difficult for anybody else, you know, if she was in hospital or perhaps in a nursing home . . .

And

> You couldn't ask her whether she needed to be wiped since

she wasn't capable of responding even if she knew what you said and she did know a lot more of what you said than . . . it appeared from her speech. So that had to be done, I mean you had to watch her because you didn't want it on her clothes and things like that.

Daughters found it painful not to be recognized by confused mothers or, in two cases, to be called 'mother' by their mothers. One reported a young child visitor also mistaking her mother for the 'child': 'He turned to my mother and said, ''Your mummy will take me to the bus.'' He thought I was the mother.'

The considerable aggression exhibited by three of the confused mothers was compared to that of a small child 'a little below the tantrum age', although in two cases it went beyond this to the point where the mother threw cups of tea at her daughter and pulled curtains off the rails, or in the other case behaved threateningly: 'One evening I was a bit scared and I did prop a chair against my bedroom door 'cos I felt she was in a funny mood and might come in with a knife in her hand or something like that.' Two respondents reported that their mothers were susceptible to huge mood changes: 'People who came in always saw the sweet side of her. She wasn't always like that with me.' The other, a married woman, attempting to give her mother semi-care at a distance, told the story of how she and her husband arrived at her mother's house to do some decorating and found her distraught: 'She was in a dreadful state. She thought she had just moved.' After the decorating was completed, 'I offered to stay on and she became so unpleasant as was her wont . . . that I couldn't. ' Two days later her mother was found wandering, but by the time the daughter arrived the next morning, 'She looked so normal that I was furious. She was delighted to see me.'

One respondent felt it necessary to emphasize to the interviewer that looking after someone with dementia did constitute caring and was a very difficult task: 'Though that's not caring . . . in the way you're thinking normally, nevertheless it's a very special kind of care . . . because it's so much more wearing than caring for bodily illnesses . . . you see you can't always understand what makes them tick.' The fact that it should be thought necessary to explain caring for the confused elderly in this way is perhaps indicative of the lack of understanding generally about dementia.

The onset of senile dementia often went unrecognized by the carer. One woman reported that her mother complained about eyesight and hearing problems for a period of some five years, but increasingly it seemed to the daughter that these were insufficient explanations for her mother's changed behaviour. It was only during tomato picking at the end of the five-year period that she became convinced there was something seriously wrong when her mother appeared not to know what she was doing with the green tomatoes. Another described how her mother could not read or tell the time but could still get by quite well in superficial conversation for some years. Regrets were expressed about not reaching an understanding of the condition sooner: 'I used to think sometimes that she was just playing on me. If only I'd had the understanding at the time it would have made her life better as well.' The study by Levin, Sinclair, and Gorbach (1983) makes clear that guilt about initial lack of understanding and about subsequent behaviour is common among carers of the confused elderly.

Strange behaviour patterns coupled with an inability to communicate often made carers impatient:

> She was always fairly amenable, she didn't really make demands. But she got so unlike herself at the end, she'd adopt a moaning tone when I did things for her. She didn't really know what she was doing and I'd say, 'Mother, do you really have to make that noise', and I used to chide myself afterwards.

This respondent used to comfort herself with the thought that her mother didn't really know her, but others were very alive to the fact that in lucid moments they felt that their mothers did understand what was happening and were concerned to do all they could to help preserve their mothers' dignity:

> She was the type that she held on to her dignity and she always still liked to be nicely dressed in company, which is part of senility. She covered up . . . but while she looked normal, to outsiders, if they said to her, 'Are you warm?' or 'Are you cold?', she would just say, 'Yes', or 'No', and they would think she was actually answering their question. . . . I did try to give her a bit of dignity and tried to keep her dressed and washed and dressed her nicely, took her out every day because she had no concentration to TV, for reading, for anything.

This respondent and the one who went to considerable trouble to try and establish what her mother wanted were convinced that their mothers retained some capacity to understand and to feel hurt, which made them reluctant to commit them to an institution, where they would in all likelihood be treated as incapable of comprehension.

Dementia exerts a particular strain upon carers, first because of the particular way in which it erodes the relationship between the carer and the elderly person; second, because of the way in which it usually precludes the possibility of the elderly person co-operating in their care; third, because of the intensity of the acutely conflicting mixture of feelings of guilt, pity, impatience, and love experienced by the carer; fourth, because of the general lack of understanding among kin and community; and fifth, because of the paucity of appropriate help and guidance presently offered by professionals. We shall explore these aspects of the problem later.

All of those caring for mothers with dementia had to undertake many of the personal care tasks that also characterize care of the physically dependent, the most widely upsetting (in sixteen cases) being that of incontinence. Several respondents experienced a deep-seated repugnance at having to deal with this aspect of personal tending. Two found it embarrassing to talk about it to the interviewer. In response to a question about what she found most difficult about caring, one replied hesitantly: 'I don't know whether you could say, p'raps, one of the most unpleasant tasks was dealing with soiled clothing . . . but . . . mothers have to cope with that with young babies.' The analogy with small children was often used, sometimes by respondents who had employed it to try and quell their mothers' feelings of helplessness and embarrassment: 'She got embarrassed and I said look, you did it for me as a baby, what's the difference?' The difference was, of course, as many were able to articulate, the humiliation experienced by the elderly person and often the embarrassment and distaste felt by the carer: 'It was the incontinence that was the biggest problem. It limited the amount she could come downstairs and limited the amount she could see friends. It's the one thing people won't put up with. It's all too embarrassing.' This respondent decided she could not cope with the smell all over the house and her mother became confined largely to her bedroom: 'You have to keep them in one room, you have to contain it a little bit, you can't have it all over the house, it was my husband's home as well.'

The majority of mothers who suffered incontinence were reported by their daughters to have become depressed and dispirited: 'She got very depressed . . . that year made her very, very low, she hated it . . . it's so degrading being incontinent isn't it?' A few mothers refused, or were unable, to acknowledge it at all, which created special difficulties for the carer:

> Very often I'd get home and I'd have to carefully open the front door because it was all over the floor, so that you came in from work and you turned to and got some hot water and scrubbed the floor. 'I don't know who put it there dear, it wasn't me.' Then she'd say to me, 'But aren't you going to eat anything?'

In less extreme cases and where the daughter was engaged in full care, the problem could often be controlled at the price of eternal vigilance:

> She'd have the odd accident, perhaps, but you could perhaps manage to keep her reasonable because you could either keep taking her or sometimes you could ask her if she wanted . . . or sometimes you could tell because she went to get out of bed.

Respondents also often experienced considerable difficulty in performing what they regarded as nursing tasks, dealing with bedsores or bathing when the mother was acutely disabled. Some respondents expressed the feeling that they should not have been expected to perform such tasks for which they felt considerable distaste: 'It was impossible for me [to bathe her], I wasn't trained for anything like that, I wasn't very good with sick people.' However, some just wished that they had had more knowledge of what to do – 'how to cope with a slippery old lady in the bath' – while others felt extremely proud that they had managed to cope with difficult nursing tasks. One respondent whose mother was bedfast for three years after a stroke, managed to stop the development of bedsores with the help of friends: 'She never got them – by all of us working at it.' In some instances, when the mother had to enter an institution the carer felt that the quality of nursing care provided was inferior to that which she, an untrained person, had given.

Many carers were also at pains to stress that care consisted of considerably more than personal tending: 'Caring is not just washing them and dressing them. It's time to talk to them, unpick that knitting that's gone wrong.' Two sisters who managed to carry on working despite their mother's relatively severe incapacity and incontinence, did not get to bed until very late each night because they spent several hours each evening talking to their mother in an effort to stimulate her before starting the work of washing dirty linen and preparing for the following day. All perceived that conversation was very important to physically dependent but mentally alert mothers, but it often imposed an additional burden on a tired carer who wanted nothing more than to sit down at 8 or 9 p.m. and read or watch television. Three respondents also stressed the importance of food preparation as an integral part of care. They felt that they knew what their mothers liked and that this served to cheer them up through what were inevitably long days. 'I had to be careful how I arranged what we would have, sometimes she didn't fancy it, or I thought it would be too rich or too heavy what I was having, so it was cooking two meals.' In many ways it is these aspects of caring that while practical, best illustrate the way love and affection are integrally mixed into the labour of tending. Again, when the mother went into hospital or a nursing home, either temporarily or permanently, the carer feared that these elements of caring would go by the board. The physical toll on the carer of caring for a physically dependent mother was perhaps as great as that for those with mothers suffering from dementia, but the distress and hence stress was in a majority of cases somewhat less, largely because less damage was inflicted on the relationship between mother and daughter. However, this should not be allowed to obscure the crucial point that it is nevertheless impossible to make generalizations and that the difficulties arising from caring tasks are perceived very differently.

Just as the importance of understanding the full extent of the caring sequence stems in part from its impact on the carer's life-course expectations, so the importance of understanding the nature of the caring task is linked to the way in which carers perceive it differently. In eleven cases the interviewer perceived the burden of care to be less than was reported by the carer, and in two cases greater than was reported. Cicirelli (1983) argued that the stress experienced by carers is due to the degree of perceived parental dependency, rather than the amount of help given by the carer. However, this is to isolate one element and to miss the complexity of caring as a set of relationships. There is a danger that the needs of those perceiving their burdens to be particularly high, will not be taken as seriously. But our data strongly suggest that the daughter's perceptions of caring must be related more broadly to her life-course expectations. Six of the eleven perceiving their burden of care as greater than it was judged to have been by the interviewer, felt that their paid employment was more important than caring. Beyond the link between the way care is perceived and the carer's other priorities lies the importance of the quality of the caring relationship between mother and daughter and the importance of support the daughter receives from external sources. While the experiences of these eleven respondents were very different, none recorded a positive response in respect to all three issues. It is to these issues that we now turn.

CHAPTER 4

The mother/daughter relationship

We have suggested, without yet offering substantive evidence, that the quality of the caring and previous mother/daughter relationship is a crucial determinant of the way in which the carer approaches, responds to, and experiences the task of caring. In the case of daughters caring for their mothers, this relationship is likely, as Helen Evers (1985) has observed, to be 'fraught with ambivalence'. It is difficult to assess the quality of these relationships. A recent small-scale qualitative study (Marsden and Abrams 1987) set out to investigate whether informal mother/daughter caring arrangements were in fact characterized by warm loving relationships, and the extent to which caring imposed emotional costs. However, in the case of mothers and daughters it is doubtful whether a focus on affection or even closeness necessarily tells us much about the quality of the relationship. As we have seen, the majority of our respondents expressed some degree of affection for their mothers, in three cases despite poor early relationships, and in sixteen cases despite consistently problematic relationships during the period of caring. In many cases the mother's deterioration exerted some strain on the relationship and daughters coped with this in a variety of ways, the most common being some form of distancing. To this extent relationships became less close as a result of caring, but it is not clear that this was viewed by daughters as an 'emotional cost'. For the most part they regarded it as sad, but inevitable.

From our evidence, it seems that the quality of relationships is better assessed by the degree to which they may be considered 'supportive' or 'problematic'. Thirteen relationships remained mutually supportive throughout the caring period, seventeen were problematic throughout, and in eleven cases the relationship deteriorated from supportive to problematic. Social exchange theorists have described an ideal model of shifting reciprocity characterized by a reversal of transfers between parent and child as the parent becomes more dependent in old age (Cheal 1983). However, the relationship will only sustain its supportive character if a balance of some kind is maintained and perceived to exist by both mother and daughter (Martin 1971; Matthews 1979). Bromberg (1983) has also emphasized that mutuality is a very important indicator of successful mother/daughter relationships, the elements of which may change over time. Those caring relationships engendering most satisfaction were characterized above all by the give and take characteristic of deep companionship and mutual interdependence, which weathered the vicissitudes of physical and as far as possible of mental deterioration, much as might be expected of devoted spouses. None of the married women in our sample reported that they were able to sustain a mutually supportive relationship with their mothers; undoubtedly it is much more difficult to balance a warm relationship with an invalid mother against that with a husband and children. In addition, all but two of the mothers of the married respondents suffered at some point during the caring period from mental illness, which tends to have a more negative effect on the quality of the caring relationship than does physical deterioration.

Whether mutually supportive, companionate relationships between mother and daughter are the result of both reconciling their antagonisms in a commitment to femininity as Hess and Waring (1978) suggest, or whether they spring more simply from the shared values whose importance has been noted by Bengston and Troll (1978), by Troll, Miller and Atchley (1979), and by Smith and Self (1980), we are not in a position to say. What was striking about our thirteen cases of mother and daughter pairs who remained mutually supportive was the degree to which they seemed to have maintained their own identities and regarded each other with an affection beyond that induced by the filial bond. As three respondents put it: 'I didn't just love her because she was my mother, but I liked her as well. She was a happy person to be with.' However, it is important to recognize that profound closeness or deep affection may well accompany both supportive and problematic relationships. A recent study of the wives of oil men employed on a 2/3 weeks-on, 2/3 weeks-off shift system found that while a majority reported an increase of affection and close-ness in their relationships, the increasing intensity also gave rise to severe problems (Lewis, Porter, and Shrimpton 1988). Similarly, the interdependency that is associated with mutually supportive relationships may become problematic if it is characterized by exclusivity and both mother and daughter become overly iso-lated and immersed in each other.

Where the shifts in reciprocity were characterized more by simple role reversal than companionship and continued mutual respect, there were often more stresses and an imbalance often developed after a period during which mother and daughter battled for control over particular aspects of the household rou-tine or of personal tending tasks. Matthews (1979) has described this most clearly and sympathetically in terms of the old mother struggling to hold on to her sources of power within the family. This sort of pattern was described by all the carers whose rela-tionships with their mothers deteriorated during the period of caring, becoming increasingly problematic, and was of course linked to the process of mental and/or physical deterioration of the mother. Willmott and Young (1960) observed similar prob-lems revolving around the issue of who was to control household affairs in their early study of a London suburb, where all the cases involved mothers who had moved into the houses of mar-ried children. In her study of mothers and daughters, Lucy Rose Fisher (1986) reported that while her daughter-respondents used the term 'role reversal' to describe the changing nature of their relationships with mothers who were becoming increasingly frail, none of her mother-respondents did so. This supports the idea that the perceptions of mothers and daughters about their relationships may differ. As Fisher observes, power is rarely simply reversed, and the process of negotiation between parent and child may be protracted, destroying the existing intimacy between mother and daughter. In our sample, the process of role reversal was most protracted and wearing in households where the daughter had always lived at home.

Our data suggest that problems arise in the central caring rela-tionship chiefly from an imbalance in the relationship, with either the mother or the daughter behaving in an overly dependent, dominant, or manipulative manner. A large literature has devel-oped on the specific problems of mother/daughter relationships, which may of course be exacerbated, or at the least exposed, by the experience of caring. Simone de Beauvoir's (1966) reflections prompted by the death of her mother are a case in point. Chodorow (1978) has written at length about the issue of autonomy and attachment in mother/daughter relationships and the way in which daughters may stay closely involved with their mothers' identities, so that they never achieve a clear sense of separate identity at all, while the mother's inability to differentiate clearly between herself and her child may be destructive to the daughter's development. Neisser (1973) has observed additionally that a mother's tyrannical behaviour may hinder her daughter's development.

Seventeen of our mother/daughter relationships were problematic in some way. A majority exhibited some manipulation/domination and/or emotional dependency on the part of the mother, and a small minority dominance on the part of the daughter, usually manifested in the way she sought to control the caring relationship. As with the supportive relationships, it is not part of our project to investigate the individual psycho-social roots of these behaviours. Our evidence on these issues consists entirely of the daughter's perceptions and we asked about the early mother/daughter relationship only in general terms. From her research on seventy-five Jewish mother/daughter pairs, Bromberg (1983) concluded somewhat surprisingly that early relationships played little part in determining the quality of the relationship in later life. Our admittedly sketchy evidence is by no means so clear cut. Only five of our respondents reported poor early relationships with their mothers and all five also experienced problematic relationships while caring. However, ten whom we did not identify as having experienced problems earlier did so while caring.

Because we were reliant on the daughter's perception of the circumstances, we cannot be sure of the mother's perspective. However, it is interesting that of the eighteen who reported that their mothers did not co-operate in caring routines, almost all also experienced problematic relationships. It is hard to establish cause and effect between these two variables, but the apparent relationship between them does raise the question as to why the mother might have withheld her co-operation. Piecing together the evidence provided by daughters, it would seem that problems of ageing and fear of dying bulk large for persons being cared for, larger indeed than is probably realized by the carers or those supporting them. There is but a small literature on the feelings of those being cared for. At this stage, we can but be aware that our concept of co-operation on the part of the mother masks a further set of complex issues. We are on firmer ground with respect to the daughters themselves and will (in later chapters) consider how their behaviour relates to their priorities and expectations, as well as the extent to which the quality of their relationships is enhanced or diminished by the external support they received.

MUTUALLY SUPPORTIVE RELATIONSHIPS

'My mother and I lived together because we chose to, we liked each other . . . we shared a common home – we could laugh together . . . I was an independent person, so was my mother, we were living together, I wasn't just looking after her.' These comments from one carer who enjoyed a mutually supportive relationship with her mother before and during the period of caring bring out some of the most important elements in this sort of relationship: friendship, independence, and shared interests. One respondent made the point that her mother never treated her as a child and nor had she ever treated her mother in this way. All the completely mutually supporting relationships were between single women carers and their mothers and they often resembled the patterns of either two women of the same age sharing living accommodation, or a husband and wife. In all cases the daughter worked for some part of the period they lived together and for as long as she was able the mother cooked and kept house for the daughter. One respondent described part of the trauma of her mother's deteriorating health as having also to learn how to cook for the first time.

Thus to all intents and purposes the division of labour in the household and indeed of power was similar to the traditional one between husband and wife, with the breadwinning daughter often able to afford the same indulgences as a fond husband towards her mother's foibles as to how things should be done in the home, or over her likes and dislikes. Despite the power imbalance, these relationships may be described as mutually supportive because both parties gained from the relationship and respected and valued the contributions and competencies of the other: 'Her friends used to say, "How lucky you are A's here", and she used to say, "And she's lucky too, not having to cook a meal or mend her clothes", and it was true, it's a two-way thing!'

In two of these relationships the mother was obviously a very strong character but also very hospitable and outgoing:

> She was a very determined lady, great spirit, and she always liked to look nice and in fact always did look nice, always got her earrings in, an awful struggle sometimes because she had arthritis in her hands . . . she was very hospitable and loved people to come in . . . going out was like Muldoon's picnic going off, but she used to love it.

Another said:

> My mother was well loved . . . she was very hospitable – if someone came and she said she liked the tea, mother would give it away and I would say, 'Oh, don't give it away, I've been shopping and can't go out again', but of course it was very nice, she never lost her courtesy.

Daughters in these circumstances were of course bearing a heavier burden than would a husband in that they usually undertook all the dealings with the world beyond the home, including shopping. But it is the indulgence and appreciation of the mother that comes out most strongly in these statements. In another case after the mother had had to enter a nursing home, she was determined to have a party for her 90th birthday:

> She wanted to have a party. A service, a service of thanksgiving. But I was living in a flat. . . . 'Well,' she said, 'can't you hire a hall?' She'd thought it all out. . . . She had a little legacy as well, and she said, 'Let's spend it and have a party,' so we did, and we had 70 people . . . she lived just six weeks after that.

Supportive mothers showed an interest in their daughters' lives and work and understood the importance of their work. One respondent became very involved in her job for a number of years and remembered her mother minding that she used to come home late for supper. 'But I could always say, "What would you have done?" and she was honest enough to say the same.' Another mother would not hear of her daughter giving up her foreign holidays to stay at home and also helped behind the scenes when her daughter entertained. This mother and daughter kept their lives as independent as possible, each taking one floor in the house: 'Some mothers want their daughters there all the time talking to them, she'd be downstairs washing up which was lovely – some evenings we didn't meet until tea at 10 o'clock, maybe we wouldn't see much of each other, I think that's why it worked so well.' Another respondent retired before her mother needed any care and reported that she spent the first summer taking classes, going on trips and going into town two or three days a week so as not to 'get in mother's hair'. This period of adjustment was profoundly similar to that experienced by men on retirement.

In these cases, where a mutually supportive relationship was sustained throughout the caring period, companionship weathered the inevitable decline in the mother's ability to contribute to the running of the household and the extra burden of care falling on the daughter:

> It was good having someone else to share life with. I could still enjoy talking to her and she continued to take a vast interest in what I did. I used to enjoy giving her pleasure – making a fuss of parties and celebrations, bringing things home from holidays.

Many of these 'supportive' daughters gave their mothers devoted care but also stressed how 'co-operative' their mothers had been. This meant above all that their mothers had been 'appreciative and patient' in the face of their increased incapacity and in response to their daughters' efforts on their behalf. Three respondents commented severely on the importance of the personality of the elderly person being cared for. As one put it: 'Not every mother . . . earns a daughter.' And: 'Not all elderly are sweet. Elderly people do not become sweet, they are what they always have been and some are crotchety.'

The importance of the elderly person making a positive response to the carer's efforts was well-demonstrated in the case of a woman who had cared for both her mother and father. She nursed her mother who had Parkinson's disease for some twenty-two years, but felt that she could not do the same for her father who outlived her mother, despite 'feeling dreadful' about his admission to a nursing home. Whereas her mother had done everything she could to make caring easy, her father began to insist that she never go out and complained constantly about what was done for him. When mothers were patient and appreciative it was left to the daughter to play more of an enabling role than anything else – keeping the mother going as well and as long as possible: 'My mother was really a lovely patient. She was very contented. She was far more patient really than she was before.' And: 'I think they [this respondent cared for mother and father] appreciated so much that they could *be* at home . . . if I found it was difficult we'd work out how I could do a thing you know. Just as I worked out how I could get them [both in wheelchairs] in a car.'

The appreciation reported by some respondents was extremely touching and understandably made the carer feel that what she was doing was profoundly worthwhile:

About a week before she died, she started crying after I cleaned her and said, 'Oh thank you, thank you, I don't know how I shall ever thank you for all you've done for me', and I got her back into bed and she didn't stop crying and I said, 'Oh, come on,' and I made her a cup of tea and sat and talked to her.

RELATIONSHIPS THAT DETERIORATED

In the cases where mutually supportive relationships were rendered problematic during the course of caring, it was often reported that the mother no longer 'co-operated' in terms of expressing her appreciation. Inevitably this was often the case when the mother developed dementia. 'Until her mind started to go she'd do everything she could . . . she definitely became a different person, she could only think of herself.' This proved to be a turning point for this respondent, who felt that once her mother was no longer able to co-operate she could no longer balance the work of caring for her with that of caring for her family. In another case, the mother got to the point where she failed to recognize the people who volunteered to sit with her and refused to be left:

She was all right until her memory failed and she couldn't remember who people were. She used to be glad that Mrs M could come and sit. Then it got to the stage when we said, 'We're going to town and Mrs M will come and sit' – 'Who's Mrs M?' After that it got very difficult.

This respondent obviously found the deterioration in the quality of her relationship with her mother as a result of dementia very painful as is revealed in her tortuous description of her feelings during that period:

It kills your affection a little bit, if that's the right way of putting it. I'm afraid I did get irritable, you do feel, perhaps you don't feel, quite so close in one way, because I suppose you feel, you're getting yourself, I mean obviously if you don't really mean it, underneath you're just as much attached, but there is that bit on top where you feel she's been a bit unreasonable and she could have done this, that or the other, but perhaps she couldn't.

However, it should be noted that in one case, the quality of the mother/daughter relationship actually improved in some respects after the mother developed dementia, because the daughter felt more pity and less hostility about her caring responsibilities. This was, to say the least, atypical. In one other case, mother and daughter had been extremely interdependent although not particularly mutually supportive before the period of full care. The mother's dementia resulted in hallucinations and abusive behaviour that eventually led to hospitalization, but the daughter also reported:

Although we were very close, there were a lot of things we never talked about. There were an awful lot of no go areas and we never showed love physically. We never hugged or kissed or anything. And now it's the only way I can communicate with her. And it's since she was ill that I've hugged her and so on, which is something quite nice that came out of it in a way.

Most of these relationships failed to withstand the tensions arising from the mother's increased incapacity and inability to perform her accustomed role in the household. In relationships that were already problematic this proved an additional strain. Both Evers (1984, 1985) and Matthews (1979) have emphasized the importance that elderly women attach to maintaining some sort of control over their lives by continuing to contribute in some respect to the household, for example by babysitting, or performing some household task. One mother was reported to have maintained a large element of control over her life by hiring help and giving firm instructions as to her care.

Some theories of ageing have assumed that women do rather better in old age than men because disengagement follows more naturally from a smoother life cycle (see the review by Havighurst, Neugarten, and Tobin 1968). Kline (1975) has argued rather that women tend to experience more discontinuities in terms of their labour force participation for example, and that it is this rather than a 'smoother' life cycle that makes disengagement easier. But Harrison (1983) and Evers (1985) have rightly questioned whether ageing *is* easier for women, emphasizing the way in which women have to battle with the stereotypes of elderly women and the economic and social disadvantages that are exacerbated by old age. Our data suggest that their doubts about the conventional wisdom in respect to women and ageing are born out by the position of women who find themselves in need of care.

Five daughters reported that their mothers were upset at the thought of being a nuisance:

'She used to say, ''It's horrid for you having to do this'' ';

'She was sensitive about me having to do everything . . . she used to say, ''Oh I am a nuisance to you'' ';

'I'd planned to do so much [on retirement]. I know it distressed her. And she knew that. She voiced it to my friends. She said so many times: ''I should have died that night'' [when she had a stroke]. I said, ''Well, you didn't Mum. We've got to soldier on'' ';

'Sometimes you'd do a bit of polishing or an odd job and she'd sit there bless her heart with the tears streaming down her face and she'd say, ''Oh I can't help you'', and I'd say, ''I know you can't love. That's why I've retired'', and it did use to upset her.'

The idea of being a burden and the anxiety that they were contributing very little was obviously deeply distressing to these mothers, but their expressions of concern did little to help their carers, who might have preferred a more cheerful interchange even though it might have necessitated denying the true nature of the burden involved. Three reported keeping a particular task for the mother to do – light ironing or more usually drying up the tea things – in a genuine effort to allow them to feel that they were participating members of the household. However such participation inevitably became ritualized and while these daughters reported that 'you see she was doing her little bit', it is not clear as to how far this went in satisfying the mother. One carer who reported doing this also said that she had to tell her mother firmly: 'This is my day, you want me to do things now, I'll do it my way ... I had to be firm ... she said, "All right dear", and perhaps I'd bring her a drink after a few minutes to tone the atmosphere down.' One mother was reported to have hung on to the job of carving the joint to the end, much to her daughter's disapproval, but undoubtedly the symbolism of this task was of crucial importance to the mother. As one respondent said, it could be difficult to discuss the question of changing roles and this in and of itself could prove a source of tension.

For daughters also experienced difficulties in dealing with the process of role reversal. In one case the mother gratefully ceded household responsibilities to the daughter when the latter retired, but the respondent reported that she felt confused and uncertain when this happened. Her mother had always dominated the home front and she was not used to taking charge there. In another case, the transition did not prove fast enough for the daughter's tastes:

> She'd always reckoned to be mistress of the kitchen and I had to be the assistant, you know, at Christmastime – she had to be in charge, she had to do everything and I had to be the kitchen maid. . . . But then she got to the stage when she wasn't doing everything right and I was itching to do things but I knew I'd get ticked off if I did so I rather went off having visitors and then one Christmas ... must have been in 1976 or 1977, she was pretty far gone and ... I felt for the first time that I was in charge. She just sat back and let me do everything ... we'd been through a few years of difficult patches where she thought she was in charge but I could see she wasn't coping, well, this last Christmas I felt she was leaving everything to me and I could do it, I didn't have to consult her about everything, which reversed roles really, which happens, you know, in families a bit doesn't it?

The interviewer gained no idea of how the mother felt during that period. Depending on the strength of personality of the mother, the daughter by no means always succeeded in taking over: 'The year I retired, I was full of zeal, and thinking I must do things in the garden and pull up weeds and so forth, which she didn't like at all, she made it known that this was her garden and that I was not to be thanked for pulling things up and I gradually gave up attempting it.'

PROBLEMATIC RELATIONSHIPS

In identifying relationships as consistently problematic, we relied entirely on the daughter's perceptions of the mother's behaviour as dominant or manipulative. However, it may well not be sufficient to attribute such behaviour entirely to personality factors. We have already drawn attention to the problem of assessing the mother's difficulties and anxieties relating to her illness and changing position in the household. Similarly, the daughter may have been successfully exercising and masking a distancing mechanism when she described her mother's behaviour as dominant, manipulative or merely difficult to the interviewer. Finally, the nature of the interrelationship between these factors is very hard to assess. Our purpose is merely to indicate the complexity of the dynamic at work in the central caring relationship and the importance of understanding the carer's perception of it, if effective help is to be given to her.

Relationships that we have called problematic – in which there existed some imbalance – were usally dominated or manipulated by the mother and in almost all these cases it was also reported that the mother failed to co-operate in her care. This suggests that the two elements should be considered together. Most dominant mothers exercised their control in indirect ways. One respondent denied that her mother was a dominant character: 'She was in charge to begin with but she's not a domineering woman by a long way.' The most resentment expressed was by carers who felt that their mothers used their illness to exert power over them:

> There was the sort of occasion where I came home from work and found she'd fallen down, and she might even have a temperature . . . and I'd have great difficulty in getting her up the stairs into bed and call the doctor, and she made a complete fool of me when the doctor came and she sat up in bed and said, 'Oh, I'm very well, there's nothing the matter with me except I can't walk.'

And

> yet she always liked having an illness to control people. She

always had something wrong with her so that people had to pander to her in some way. I mean the actual horror of the multiple sclerosis she used to pretend wasn't really there.

Such attention-seeking behaviour, which might in some cases only have been exacerbated by painful and isolating illness, while in others might have been a quite new and compensatory form of behaviour resulting from illness, was extremely wearing for carers, who not surprisingly felt increasingly 'trapped' by their situation.

In some cases such feelings were worsened by the mother's attempts to control the daughter's behaviour. The most common complaint was of the mother's possessiveness: 'She wanted me to be with her all the time, which was very frustrating. She had to know where I was all the time, how long I was going to be. If I wasn't back on the dot she thought I'd had an accident.' In cases where the mother was quite able to undertake personal care tasks herself, it was this kind of behaviour which resulted in what we have identified as the semi-care tie. Four respondents reported that their mothers exercised a kind of censorship on their activities that evoked responses ranging from resentment to resigned tolerance. One mother considered it necessary for her daughter to attend funerals but not weddings, another was happy for her daughter to go out if she thought the event was worthwhile or approved of the friends. Yet another did not like her daughter's habit of writing letters on a Sunday afternoon. There was very little mention of mothers' reactions to men friends by the unmarried women. In only one case was the mother reported to have taken an active dislike to a fiancé, whom the daughter persisted in seeing but never married.

In relationships where the mother was dominant, the daughter's identity tended to be submerged in that of the mother in a manner characteristic of daughters who stay closely involved with their mothers. One reported that the local community always referred to her as 'X's daughter'. At the extreme, the daughter might actually succeed in exercising very little control over the caring situation. One respondent obviously did whatever her mother wanted until her mother could no longer make decisions, whereupon she obeyed the instructions of professionals. Dominant mothers could also be extremely dependent. We have already discussed the ways in which it was not uncommon for many of this particular generation of mothers to begin to depend on their daughters when their husbands died. Such dependence often increased with the onset of illness and the gradual falling away of the mother's friends and personal networks. In depending more and more on her daughter for all forms of interaction outside the home, the mother tended to behave in a fiercely proprietorial way within it. In some cases, an interdependence developed that tended to be more destructive than mutually supportive, the mother depending entirely on the daughter for social contact and care, which she attempted to manipulate, and the daughter wrapped up in care of the mother to whom she remained subservient. We recorded some eight cases where this sort of dynamic seemed to be at work.

For the most part, dominant mothers were also reported to be uncooperative in some or all aspects of their care, although it should be noted that of the eighteen uncooperative mothers, thirteen had developed some degree of mental illness by the end of the caring period. Most common was the refusal to consider the possibility of someone else caring. The mother would either refuse point blank to have a sitter, or to go into a home while the daughter went on holiday. However, the mother's view is important here and was acknowledged by two carers who experienced mutually supportive relationships with their mothers. They reported that their mothers would only have sitters they knew. As one pointed out, seen from the mother's perspective this was understandable: 'You can't just . . . I remember a friend saying any time you want help . . . and I said, "Come and meet my mother," and she said, "No, no." That's no good, they must have the patience to learn, they can't just come in and do everything.' This respondent enjoyed a mutually supportive relationship with her mother and recognized instantly that granny-sitting was in no way comparable to babysitting in that an elderly incontinent or severely disabled woman would naturally feel reluctant to spend an evening or a longer period of time with a total stranger. In the case of the mother with senile dementia cited earlier, sitters were refused when the mother no longer recognized them.

It should also be acknowledged that respondents were sometimes too involved in their role as carers to take a break. One daughter attempted a holiday in Wales, but was called back on the first day because her mother was so distressed: 'I still felt obliged to come back even though they got her into a nursing home, although everyone said don't.' Another reported:

> In the event it [respite care] was supposed to be for nearly a fortnight, but I got her out after a week. I wasn't awfully keen on the idea. I wasn't keen on the idea to start with to be honest with you . . . she wasn't happy about it, but she went quite willingly because she said I wanted a break, but I knew she wasn't happy in there so I got her out after a week.

This episode occurred in the year before her mother died and was the only occasion she tried it. Another daughter described the way her mother would go to her sister's for a break each year for a fortnight:

> She didn't altogether enjoy it truth to tell. I used to say, 'Well you could stay another week.' 'Don't you dare suggest it,' she'd say. . . . She didn't get the consideration – they would sort of leave her and perhaps go out and not explain when they'd be back or where they were going.

This respondent effectively colluded with her mother to cut visits to her other daughter short. In large part this was because she valued her mother's company so highly.

Daughters who became extremely involved in the work of caring for their mothers often tended to think that no one else could care properly for them. In part this related to the combination of love and labour that characterizes all caring, but was substantially complicated for our sample by the mother/daughter relationship and the failure of many daughters to achieve autonomy. Another respondent who enjoyed a very supportive relationship with her mother faced the issue of jealousy squarely: 'When my mother went to my sister she'd be far more spoiled than the rest of the year.' Her mother told a friend that she was looking forward to going for this reason and the friend asked the respondent whether she did not find this unfair: 'I said it's good that she be spoiled, but I can't do it all year.'

Nevertheless daughters also reported what would appear to be a variety of more manipulative behaviours by their mothers:

> She was so unpredictable you couldn't plan anything, you could never say next Saturday we'd just go out, because you could guarantee that Saturday she'd suddenly have one of her

bad days and on her bad days she really did look dreadful, but on the next day she'd be all pinky and perky again.

Another respondent who was engaged in a demanding schedule of part-time full care was never able to take a break: 'Though she knew that I really ought to have a rest, her fear of my being away from this place sort of overrode . . . though she knew I should have gone away and she admitted it – but the fear was stronger.' This mother also tended to impede her daughter's departure for work in the morning by often not quite making it to the toilet.

Five respondents also described demands made by their mothers that significantly increased their caring burden. A mother who suffered from multiple sclerosis refused to sleep downstairs which meant that the daughter had to lift her legs up every stair when she went to bed. This example demonstrates the great difficulty in drawing the line between the elderly person's desire to remain in control and the convenience of the carer. Another respondent reported that even when she asked her mother not to do something for her own safety she still went ahead and did it: 'Even if you said it nicely, she thought, "Mmm, telling me what to do".' The respondent thought that this was purely a matter of her mother still thinking of her as a child and not wishing to take instructions from her. Undoubtedly this was a part of it, but the mother also probably feared giving up control to her daughter.

One mother refused to accept aids that might have made things easier:

You see they measured up the bath for a bath seat, she said she'd like that – well then she tried it out and said it was no earthly good and so we sent it off. We got her a walking aid which she would use only to go from the lounge to the toilet . . . anything that was given to help her be more independent was no good. I mean she really did like everybody being at her beck and call and having people run round.

Another mother who relied on her daughter for most aspects of personal care actually began to do a lot more for herself after entering an old people's home. Two respondents reported that their mothers refused to have home helps, one because the housework had to be done in the morning and the home help came in the afternoon, and the other because she would not let a stranger into the house.

In our sample the extent of lack of co-operation of one form or another by mothers was striking. This is something that is mentioned only in passing in the study by Levin, Sinclair, and Gorbach (1983) of the supporters of the confused elderly and that needs more extensive examination. More home helps, bathing attendants, or respite care will not be effective unless help is also provided in persuading the elderly person (and sometimes the carer) to use them. Our data do not provide direct information as to why mothers acted in the way they did. However we can make some suggestions that may be worthy of further investigation. The most striking element shared by a majority of non-cooperating mothers was that of fear, whether of disease, death, or some aspect of ageing. The mother who would not admit her lapses in memory, or the one who would not be seen outside in her wheelchair, were in all probability experiencing difficulty in coming to terms with their infirmities.

Daughters were sometimes sensitive to particular aspects of this more general phenomenon. One, for example, concurred in her mother's objection to the bathing service because she felt that it was wrong for elderly people to be stripped down without due regard for their modesty. But carers seemed to be much less aware of the significance of their mothers' fears of disease and death. One mother was exceptional in talking to her daughter freely about her death and seemingly played a major role in helping her to come to terms with it. More common was the reluctance to let the daughter out of her sight for fear that she would have an accident, leaving the mother to fend for herself. This was the overriding preoccupation of the possessive mother cited above, who wanted to know where her daughter was and how long she would be. The respondent who felt she must return from her holiday when her mother was reported to be distressed said that her mother always insisted on accompanying her:

> I think she was frightened if I had an accident. I often teased her: 'Yes, you want to come to see if I have an accident and you want to be there.' It was no fun for her. Quite often it would be quite hot in the boiling sun [waiting in the car] and she'd complain about that so you couldn't win.

This daughter felt totally trapped by her caring responsibilities and her only way of exerting herself was by mocking her mother's fears, thus contributing further to an already bad relationship.

Another mother suffering from cancer behaved in a similar fashion:

> I think it was fear the whole time. She made me promise that I wouldn't leave her. We fixed up a baby alarm so that I could hear her at nights and sometimes I would sleep on the recliner with her because she just did not want to be left and that was the most trying thing.

Fear of death and fear of institutionalization became overwhelming in such cases. Both these respondents recognized this and one responded sympathetically. We feel that in the other instance the daughter strongly resented her mother's constant checking on her movements, without either asking or perceiving why her mother may have behaved in this way. Some counselling might have served both carer and her mother well in this situation. At a less traumatic level, uncooperative mothers may also have resented and feared losing control over their domain in the manner of the one quoted above who very reluctantly ceded supervision of the Christmas festivities to her daughter.

Some daughters fought back against overly dominant and uncooperative mothers, as in the case of the respondent who teased her mother about her fear of being left. Much more common was the effort to exert some control via the tasks of caring. One respondent, a former nurse, reported that she had 'geared up for this geriatric situation'; to all intents and purposes her mother was another case and she saw it as something of an accomplishment that she had chivvied her along and kept her going. Another found that she could take the upper hand for the first time when her mother developed dementia.

> I'd always considered myself to be a bit stupid and a bit less intelligent than most of the people around. Now suddenly my mother was being very stupid so I could sort of – I mean this is all unformed but I'm sure that's the sort of instinct it was – to lord it over her. I was suddenly more powerful than she was.

These two cases represent the extreme, but in some nine others there was evidence of the daughter exhibiting flashes of determination to impose her will, albeit unsystematically, on the situation, often treating the mother as a child. In the case of one pair of sisters looking after their mother who suffered from Alzheimer's Disease, one distanced herself from the situation by treating her mother as a little old lady removed from the mother she had known, while the other babied her. The mother seems to have resented the latter treatment, with the result that the daughter's behaviour made the mother's lack of co-operation worse.

The intensity of the caring relationship between mother and daughter, combined with both the tension arising from tending a loved one whose physical and mental state is deteriorating and a deterioration in a relationship which might already have been problematic, is bound to give rise to a conflicting mixture of feelings in the carer and to a variety of strategies to deal with the situation. Five respondents said that they felt both resentful and protective towards their mothers. One of these enjoyed a mutually supportive relationship with her mother but resented the constraints caring placed on her career. Another with an extraordinarily manipulative mother described her mother's uncooperative conduct in detail, but still defended her mother:

> She had quite a sense of fun. [But] one psychiatrist said, and I was quite hurt on her behalf, 'She's dull and demanding.' That was his verdict, and off he went. In a way she does appear to be dull. I don't know whether she was dull as a young woman. I don't know whether her marriage had a lot to do with it.

In other cases the mixture was more resentment and pity: 'As I said I was really very sorry for her. I thought, you know, she's had a very raw deal, one, losing my father, and then getting this horrible disease, but I also resented the hold she had over me.'

Mixed feelings such as these lead very easily to guilt. Almost all our respondents talked of feeling guilty, most often in respect to their perceived failure to live up to an ideal of caring that involved endless patience and affection, and sometimes in respect to a retrospective concern that they had not given sufficient priority to their mothers in struggling to balance caring with their other responsibilities and activities. This same respondent spoke of the tremendous demands her mother made on her and the way she felt about it:

I mean for one thing after my father died she said she wouldn't have any social activities unless I was invited too, and the other side of that was I shouldn't have any social activities unless she was invited and you know I resented that, but at the time I felt that this was unreasonable of me to resent it.

Another respondent distinguished between what might be termed a ritual or surface guilt and a deeper feeling:

I think it's very easy to say, 'Oh I feel so guilty when I go out', but I think it is a very superficial guilt we all feel. I wouldn't say guilt is my overriding feeling when thinking of mother and I don't think it's that that stops you going out. You feel rotten if you go out and leave them but you also know you're going out to do essential shopping or something.

A good example of 'ritual guilt' was provided by another respondent who, when asked how she felt about caring generally, said that she felt she had not done either more or less than she should have done, but later said: 'Well, you never feel you've done enough for people of course. You keep thinking back, I should have done more. I should have held my tongue. I should have done better.' This respondent did experience 'real guilt', albeit unarticulated, in relation to her sister who battled to bring up three children, did not enjoy her mother's favour, and whose financial circumstances were vastly inferior. Nevertheless for many the feeling that they should have done more, or not snapped at a senile and/or disabled mother, were matters of genuine remorse and sources of guilt. One respondent was worn down by trying to contain her mother's faecal incontinence, a 'nightmare' for her, but a game for her mother. She used to shout at her mother who could not argue back, and then feel guilty. She would then say to her mother: ' "Oh you don't want to take any notice of my bad temper, I am sour and bad tempered and I love you", and she understood . . . and that was nice.' In the case of a pair of sisters who cared for their mother, one expressed and obviously felt considerably more guilt than the other. Significantly this sister was the one who received virtually no support from her workplace and who also felt guilty about not meeting her obligations to her employers.

To some extent painfully conflicting emotions and guilt could be lessened if the daughter managed to distance herself from the

mother. Obviously those who were immersed in the caring relationship could not. One commented she could not be like a nurse
and 'shut it off'. Many achieved only a superficial distancing,
which nevertheless made the situation more bearable. A variety
of strategies were pursued to this end. One of the most common
was to see the mother as a 'little old lady, not my mum'. In the
case of the two sisters cited above, the one who did not experience such extreme feelings of guilt reacted in this way while her
sister tended to 'baby' her mother, who resisted. Treating the
mother objectively, as a 'case', was a similar strategy. Sometimes
the respondent suddenly switched to the use of the second and
third person plural in talking about her mother:

> You'd get up two or three times in the night and you'd think,
> I've got to be up at twenty to six in the morning and you're
> wandering around and you're bitterly cold, and then trying to
> get a filthy dirty nightdress off without getting it over her, you
> and everything else, and she's turning round and hitting you
> and saying I hate you. . . . You usually managed to get them
> changed but it was difficult.

Another who was a nurse and who certainly approached caring
for her mother as another case, consistently employed the use of
the third person plural: 'They get dirtier as they get older. They
can't be bothered.' Four respondents achieved a certain degree
of geographical distance within the house, including the respondent who encouraged her mother to stay in her bedroom
because of her incontinence. Two managed to find ways of
cutting out the immediate problems caused by the mother's
condition. One simply did not let herself think about whether the
gas taps had been turned on, closed her bedroom door at night
and ignored her mother's wandering and did not insist that she
wash when she became averse to water.

Some efforts to achieve distance from the person being cared
for, which became necessary for most carers as they faced the
prospect of their mother's death, were rather more successful. A
respondent who enjoyed a supportive relationship with her
mother started to plan what she would do after her mother died:
'A year before she died I started planning what I'd do when
she'd gone. It sounds awful but I even planned what I'd put in
this room, you have to, you have to make yourself think there'll
be a life afterwards.' This was in fact a very wise strategy. The

death or institutionalization of the mother was more often than not profoundly traumatic for carers.

Because our central caring relationships were all comprised of mothers and daughters, they gave rise to particular kinds of tensions. These may be linked to the issue of autonomy and attachment, and whether the daughter succeeds in achieving a balanced relationship with her mother or whether the mother remains dominant, in which case the mother's behaviour is likely to take on a more manipulative flavour as she becomes more dependent on her daughter for personal tending. On the other hand the issue of balance or imbalance in the caring relationship, the degree to which the elderly person co-operates in his/her care and the way carers deal with feelings of ambivalence and guilt are relevant to all caring relationships. It is likely that it is as hard for a spouse as a daughter to distance him/herself from an intensive caring situation as from a relationship that is deteriorating in quality. The wider implications of our examination of the central caring relationship are important because unless something of the complicated dynamic that characterizes this relationship is understood, it will be impossible to determine an appropriate form of support acceptable to both carer and person being cared for.

CHAPTER 5

Carers' extra-caring lives

The only carer in our sample who is currently being cared for commented in the following way about different perspectives of the carer and the person being cared for: 'I think in other words, when you're being cared for your priorities are completely different from those when you're not being cared for. You've got to change your attitude towards life and everything.' As we indicated in the last chapter, part of the explanation for a mother's uncooperative behaviour may lie in the fears induced by her physical deterioration and in the fact that these may not be adequately recognized by her carer. Similarly, many of the problems the daughter experiences in the caring relationship are attributable to her fight to balance priorities between work and caring, or other family and caring, as well as to tensions arising from the internal dynamic between mother and daughter.

PAID WORK AND CARING

We have already observed, for example, that none of the married women enjoyed a mutually supportive relationship with their mothers throughout the caring period, and this undoubtedly reflects the degree of tension they experienced in balancing their other family commitments. Similarly, of the ten respondents who felt work to be their most important priority, a substantial majority experienced problematic relationships with their mothers and also perceived the burden of care to be greater than that perceived by the interviewer. Litwak's (1985) study of informal networks found that married women who also went out to work experienced less conflict in respect to caring than single women, and suggested that this might be due in part to the fact that married women were giving help to the elderly at times in the life cycle that did not compete with work goals. However, it is impossible to generalize in this way. The married woman respondent who had planned to care for her mother, but not for another ten years or so, and who had a mortgage commitment that depended on two incomes, would not have fitted this description. Litwak also assumes that married women have no career goals. While for the most part this was true of the married women in our sample, recent research (Joshi 1984) shows that it is unlikely to be true for the next generation of 'women in the middle'. Other studies (e.g. Fengler and Goodrich 1979) have suggested that the double burden of work and caring may prove too great. Again, this will depend both on whether there are other family members – husband and children – to be cared for, and on the carer's expectations and priorities. Brody and Schoonover (1986) have shown how married women caring for widowed mothers may strive to balance paid work and home commitments. In most of the cases they discuss, the care provided by working daughters was equivalent to that provided by non-working daughters. However, the incapacity of mothers of working daughters was less than that of non-working daughters, and as it increased, so many daughters were forced to reduce or give up their paid employment.

All but one of our respondents had a work history. Thirteen continued to work throughout the period of caring, of these two were married. Eleven stopped working many years before beginning to care for their mothers, three for reasons of marriage and childbirth, two because of their own poor health, and two in order to look after their fathers. Three retired before commencing caring, eight retired in order to assume the burden of full care and a further five either worked part-time or took a less demanding job. All those who worked throughout the caring period experienced some conflict between commitment to their jobs and to caring. A majority found caring to be an impediment to their careers, but some would have preferred to become full-time carers. A similar mix of attitudes was also true of those retiring from work or reducing their paid work to care. Among those who were not engaged in paid employment when they started to care for their mothers, two, both married, said they would have liked to return to work had they not begun to care for their mothers.

Not all employed carers had to face acute conflict between paid work and caring; either the mother's condition made it possible to continue working reasonably easily, or the carer managed to get sufficient help to tide her over the period of full care. But for thosewho did have to face making a choice, their decision depended at least in part on age and financial security. For the women who were working and in their forties or younger when caring commenced, there was little thought of giving up work if it could possibly be avoided. In the case of one of the pairs of sisters caring, the sister with the better job (and pension prospects) kept her job while the other retired to care. Another woman who relied entirely on her wage packet said: 'You've got to face it, you either do one thing or the other.' She gave up work and hoped the state would provide. In fact she suffered considerable hardship from her mother being refused the attendance allowance (see Appendix C) on her first application. Of those faced with the issue of whether to let work or caring take precedence, only one decided, in consultation with her mother and with great reluctance, that the latter should enter a home. Those who had to give up work to care or who, in one case, took unpaid leave to do so, suffered financially and this, as will be seen later (in Chapter 8), created a legacy of bitterness.

The majority of those who continued to work did so because they found it both fulfilling and a necessary counterbalance or even escape from caring. As one put it, going to work was a mental 'release', even though the journey was tiring: 'I think if I'd been with my mother 24 hours a day I'd have gone mad.' Another gave up everything except her job to care because of her fears regarding pension rights and financial security, but also, it may be sensed, for the alternative structure that work provided. Her job provided both a different rhythm and made an entirely different set of demands on her:

> My social life went to the wall, it's true, but not my working life . . . I was adamant about that, come hell or high water I thought I was entitled to that . . . and I felt that I was completely justified in standing my ground there and I did.

The justification she used to her mother was economic, to which her mother could not object, as she did to her daughter going out socially. Other single women carers made a similar choice between carrying on working and social life for similar reasons. One took up penfriends because writing letters was something she could do at home, whereas she could not get out to see friends.

Even when the respondent decided she wanted to keep her job, the double strain could prove formidable. This was particularly true when the employer was unsympathetic. Indeed our evidence suggests this to have been a key factor. Where employers were flexible it was usually beneficial for respondents to keep their jobs: 'I had a very accommodating Head who let me have time off when I needed it', and: 'I had a marvellous boss, he didn't mind if I was sometimes late in the morning when her arthritis was bad.' The contrast with women who were allowed no leeway at all, and who took their holiday leave as and when necessary to look after their mothers, is acute: 'Our leave year ends in March which is unfortunate because it meant that I couldn't take any holiday in the summer in case I had to use it in the winter' (when her mother was particularly susceptible to bronchitis, requiring careful nursing). In the case of one of the pairs of sisters it was striking that the one who got support from her employer in terms of leave experienced much less guilt and stress than the other who was forced to take her three weeks' holiday in the form of half-days when her mother had a stroke:

> They wanted people to arrange illnesses to happen in the holidays. I had to really hide. I used to run home in the lunch time . . . and that was hard. . . . They had no idea. You were a nuisance you see because you interfered with *work* . . . in a commercial world you're *money* to them . . . and most of them were men so they've never had to look after anyone, their wives have done it, or their sisters or somebody.

Conflicting priorities could thus give rise as much to guilt as to conflicting feelings. This respondent felt guilty about leaving her mother to go to work *and* about not meeting her employer's expectations. Another respondent also had to cycle three miles home at lunch time to check on her mother, but while she found this a considerable physical strain, her employer's sympathetic attitude enabled her to carry on. In the case of the other pair of sisters who cared together for their mother, one did give up work to care and became extremely isolated and depressed as a result. The difficulties experienced by this woman who had no desire to stay at home demonstrates the dangers of what Land and Rose (1985) have called 'compulsory altruism'. Even in a case where the respondent took early retirement from her secretarial job quite willingly, she found that she did miss the work: 'I missed the contact with men [nervously]. They always used to have a laugh and a joke.' This respondent ended up immersing herself in caring for her mother to the detriment of her own mental health. Two respondents spoke strongly about the importance of their job both in taking their minds off caring and in providing an anchor when their mothers died or were institutionalized.

Those women who were committed to their jobs and found work more fulfilling than caring also tended to report that they had missed opportunities, particularly for promotion, either because they could not pursue additional training or because they were not mobile. One of the married women respondents whose re-entry to the workforce was additionally delayed by caring for her mother as well as her children felt that she'd 'lost five years which I don't know if I'll ever catch up with'. On the other hand in two cases respondents reported that they had made career sacrifices to care, but it was by no means clear from either the chronology of their narratives or the way in which they talked about their aims and expectations that this was actually so. One who gave up a job as a nurse, which she referred to with some pride, did so at a time when she also reported her own health to have been very poor. She seems later to have transferred her full attention to the welfare of her mother. In the other case, the respondent blamed her parents' condition for her failure to have made a career on the stage and, after she had become a teacher, for her failure to move south to take a better job. She repeated several times that: 'People say that I made a choice [to care], but it wasn't that clear cut.' When feelings of love and obligation are considered, this is certainly true, but this respondent's account also revealed both considerable insecurity about her abilities and an indecisiveness that suggests that she too may have in retrospect attached a disproportionate significance to caring in accounting for her failure to meet her own goals. It is very difficult for interviewers to make judgements about such possible *ex post facto* rationalizations.

However, in both these cases perhaps the most important message conveyed by the carer was the struggle to keep an identity separate from that of her mother and from that of 'carer':

Keep your own identity, that's the main thing. My friends never think of me as a carer. Not to have been caring would have been like going to the moon, but it would have been terrible to think caring was all there was in my life.

The vast majority of respondents were happy to be considered carers, although they may also have stressed other activities as being important, but the minority of our sample who wished to be identified with a career experienced extreme tension arising from the conflict between this desire and the work of caring, which, as they were aware, earned them little place in the world at large.

The strain experienced by these women was qualitatively very different from the rather larger number who said they would willingly have given up work sooner had there been more financial help available. The married woman whose family suffered financial hardship because of her mother's need for care, which happened some ten years before she thought it would, commented: 'If I'd known about the attendance allowance from the very beginning, I could perhaps have given up the job a little earlier so my own health would have been saved by that, it would have been easier for me.' Another reported: 'Nothing . . . would have persuaded me not to give up my job because I was very anxious that my mother's last months of life [she died of cancer] should be as she wanted them.' However, her mother had very little by way of a pension and she was only allowed a leave of absence without pay by her employers. Thus for two months she and her mother lived on £7 a week (in 1972).

UNPAID WORK AND CARING

Married women faced the possibility of balancing caring for their mothers with caring for a family and paid employment. In fact only two married women continued to work throughout the period of caring. In one case the respondent only looked after her mother on a co-resident basis for a matter of months, after which her mother decided that she would prefer to battle on by herself. The mother's house had been deemed unsuitable, but she preferred it and her independence to her daughter's flat, which, because it had no lift, effectively rendered her housebound. This situation was atypical, not least because the daughter clearly preferred the company of her mother to that of her husband, to whom she referred disparagingly. While prepared to care for her mother under any circumstances, the respondent also preferred that she return home where she could be visited, enabling the respondent to get away from her husband. In the other case, the respondent had only managed to go back to work after childbirth because her mother had acted as babysitter, but she made a clear decision that she could not sacrifice her earnings in order to look after her mother:

> Someone said I should have given up my job and looked after my mother. [What did you say?] I said well I have three young children and if I give up work my children would miss a lot. And even though she is my mother my first duty is to my children, so why should I give up my job? We would have been very hard pushed. So I said all right, I give up my job. Six months later my mother dies. What happens? I've given up a good job, a pensionable job. So no one could answer that. [In retrospect do you still think this?] I think so yes. Obviously when you get married and have children your first duty is to them. Say I had a mentally handicapped child, that's different, I would have to care for the child. But being my mother who, shall I say, had the best years of her life, she had a very good life and I didn't think it was fair to do that, to make such a big sacrifice. My brother suggested that to me. He suggested I give up my job. I said why don't you give up your job?

This respondent was nevertheless very torn between her love for her mother and her own family and spoke of having 'to choose between one kind of duty and another kind of duty. That was very difficult. I had to choose to let her go [into a home] [tears].'

The conflict between affection for mother and affection for family, and between obligation to mother and obligation to family is central to the caring experience of most married women. The two kinds of caring, both central to the concept of femininity, are not necessarily compatible. Another respondent who did have a mentally handicapped child and who had not worked since her marriage also felt this same conflict. She had lived with her mother until her marriage at age 33. Her mother had been divorced while the respondent was still a child, she was an only child and the bond between mother and daughter was strong. In retrospect, the respondent said that she would not have taken her mother in had she known that it would be for eleven years and that her mother would develop dementia. In this instance there was no conflict between work and caring, but when the mother got to the stage where she could not be left, a period that lasted some four years, the daughter reported that she consciously

decided that husband and children had to come first and in the
end the decision was made to seek a home for the mother. In
another case the daughter's allegiance to her mother proved so
strong that she moved into her mother's house to care for her
and her husband visited on weekends. Apparently the daughter's
house was not altogether suitable for caring for the mother, but
there was no clear practical reason for the daughter choosing this
particular course, which imposed tremendous strain on her
marriage.

The most striking aspect of married women's efforts to balance
care for their mothers against caring for husbands and children
was the way in which they strove to keep life as 'normal' as possible for their own families. This entailed assuming the whole
burden of care themselves and keeping it as unobtrusive as possible: 'You feel all the responsibility is yours. They're only doing
it just to help you, but the whole responsibility is mine. It was a
big burden, a very big burden.' Most married women respondents made enormous efforts to carry on cooking the same sort of
meals and to keep the same household routine. One, whose
mother became senile and incontinent within a week of suffering
a stroke described the enormity of the task: 'It was a struggle. It
was all so new, so sudden. It just took all the time, there was just
nothing else I could do. I just managed to do the washing – bung
it in the machine. There were the shirts piling up.' This kind of
reaction stemmed in part from the desire to keep the home in
order. Only two respondents, both single, spoke of the necessity
to reconcile themselves to a lower standard of domestic cleanli-
ness and tidiness. The majority, single and married, seemed to
have waged an unequal struggle to maintain high standards of
housewifery in the face of an increasing volume of work, especially laundry, and less time. In essence, most carers found that
the role of houseworker and that of carer tended to conflict with
one another, just as caring for an elderly mother was not necessarily compatible with caring for other family members.

In addition, wives seemed to have worried constantly that the
caring routine might impinge on their husbands:

I used to think I was doing an injustice to him. Our time was
running out, suppose Mama lives 'til 90. Then what happens?
. . . [What did he think?] He used to be very bitter – well not bitter – he was an orphan so he never knew the love of parents

... although he was marvellous with her, absolutely marvellous.

This husband started to help with the cooking, but the respondent felt very much that this was her work and should not be done by others. All but one expressed worries about the lack of free time they had to spend with husbands because of the work of caring: 'That was the worrying thing really. I knew it wasn't fair on J. But what could I do short of putting her in a home which I didn't want to do?'

There was no sense among our married respondents of sharing the tasks of caring with other family members, particularly husbands. Husbands received an excellent press and in a majority of cases seem to have been genuinely supportive, but none was reported to have helped in the actual work of caring. Respondents mentioned the importance of having someone to talk to, one couple got into the habit of taking the dog for a short walk each evening so that the wife could let off steam. But apart from that the only practical help mentioned was the husband's practice of coming in from work and talking to the mother for half an hour, which enabled the wife to talk to the children and get on with preparing the supper. Husbands undoubtedly also suffered some strain. One who always made a point of talking to the mother when he got in suffered from asthma, which worsened considerably during the period of caring. But married women expected very little of their husbands, being grateful above all if they didn't complain: 'He felt it was a shame that we were restricted, but as I say, he never complained.' This husband came in after the mother had retired to her room at night and left in the morning before the respondent began the routine of getting her mother up, and so played no part in the everyday caring task at all. Wenger (1984) reported that carers received instrumental support in caring from their husbands, but looked for expressive support elsewhere. If anything our findings tend to suggest the opposite. Litwak (1985) concluded that women who incorporated their husbands into the work of caring experienced greater stress. None of our respondents actively sought to enlist their husbands on a systematic basis, but our findings confirm that women believe they have failed in some way if they do not manage to keep the household routine going smoothly, or if husbands have to lend a hand. Stress and guilt arose not so much from a simple competition between the demands of the husband and the demands of the mother (although this was certainly a factor), as from the sense that respondents felt they had to take complete responsibility both for the caring task and for any effects caring might have on family life. One respondent commented that she felt she was always 'in the middle between the family and my mother. I was pulled both ways', and she felt extremely guilty when the strain caused her to snap at either party.

Children also had to be 'fitted in', but respondents did not lay as much emphasis on the tensions they experienced in respect to responding to their children's needs as well as those of their mothers. However, only seven of our respondents had children living at home during the caring period, which limits the conclusions we can draw. Two respondents regretted the lack of spontaneity in family life that resulted from caring, and both used the same example of a wedding invitation: 'It was so difficult to organise sitters and the family. If there was a wedding – I had to leave meals for them [mother and sitter] and see they'd got everything they wanted, then think about what we needed, did we need a new outfit? Get the children organized.' And: 'If there was a wedding in the family very often we couldn't do it . . . [it was] a massive effort.' Nor could the family take advantage of a sunny Saturday to go out for the day.

Many single respondents felt that conflicts between teenage children and an elderly grandmother would prove insuperable. Certainly one of our respondents said that she was glad her mother had come to live in the household when the children were very small because that way she had always been a part of their lives. This respondent felt that it would be very difficult to change the routine of older children. In another family space problems meant that a teenage daughter had to share her room with the grandmother, which proved impossible when the grandmother developed dementia and became incontinent. The psychological effects of such situations on children have not been accorded much consideration. One respondent reported that her son had been very adversely affected: 'She'd been with us all his life . . . but he wouldn't go to see her in hospital or in the home. [Did he ever talk about it at all?] No, not to my knowledge.' The older daughter was reported to have given up nursing because she hated geriatrics. This respondent had struggled hard to maintain as normal a domestic routine, while caring for her mother, as possible and in so doing may have effectively denied the impact it was having on her children. Another respondent cared for a very dominant mother who had little patience with children:

> I was in the middle a lot of the time with the children. Protecting them because she had quite high expectations of them and if they didn't come up to expectations she would tend to tell them off without consulting me. . . . My daughter, who's quite a placid character, just took it in her stride, but the younger one, he's quite a different kettle of fish altogether, he very much resented her being around the whole time.

As the mother deteriorated (with cancer), the son could not cope and was eventually relieved of his duty of visiting his grandmother.

Whereas respondents tended to be grateful if husbands visited their mothers, children were usually expected to consider their grandmother and to visit her. In the case of the respondent with the mentally handicapped son, the visits served to defuse tension in the household:

> He would go up and chat to her and of course he would boss her around, which was quite funny, if he thought she was going to get out of bed and do something he'd say, 'You mustn't do that Nanny', and then he'd come and tell us, so really he was quite a little messenger at times.

No one else in the household could have played this role with impunity. However to an outside observer it seems that children may be vulnerable in such situations; certainly the effect of family care for the elderly on children is something that merits longitudinal study.

A LIFE OF ONE'S OWN?

Much of the difficulty experienced by married and single women in fitting the work of caring into their lives stemmed from the fact that caring seemed to fill all the available time, leaving very little for husbands and children or for non-work activities and a life of their own. In large part this was because caring for a physically or mentally ill person does require many hours of grinding routine work each day (see pp. 38–49). Any carer who got her mother up and dressed, went to work, came home, fed and bathed her mother, did the laundry and a few other household chores, had very little opportunity for social activities. And apart from the tasks of personal tending, many who went to work all day thought they should keep their mothers company as much as they could in the evenings: 'I couldn't leave her. I used to think, "Well I don't know, she's been on her own all day", you know, that you are left completely on your own.' Many felt acutely the lack of any life beyond work, or caring for children and caring for mother: 'Well you do think sometimes, "Oh dear", you wish you could get on and do a few other things because you're completely tied to it . . . you really have got to devote all your time and interests to their interests.' Another said: 'You don't go anywhere, you don't do anything, so you don't spend much. It's like being in service, I got one evening off, Wednesday evening and one afternoon a month, on Sunday [when she had a sitter prepared to come in].' This was said with a little laugh and no trace of bitterness, but the comparison with pre-war domestic service is telling. Another respondent who was considerably better off financially said: 'It was just not having one half hour to oneself. It was being a sentry. You can't go off duty until you get relief.' The crucial difference here was that the respondent could afford to pay for regular sitters.

In addition to the *reality* of the constraints on their time experienced by carers, many *felt* that they shouldn't go out 'in case something happened'. The phrase, 'you never knew what you might find' was frequently used by respondents. Some daughters felt a deep obligation to stay with their mother, especially overnight. One articulated her fear that if she went away her mother might die. The sense of constant responsibility and awareness of the guilt they would feel should anything happen in their absence effectively tied the vast majority of carers. For example, the respondent who could afford to pay for regular sitters reported that she had not hired as much help as she could have for fear that something might happen while she was away. These feelings constrained carers throughout the whole caring sequence. During long periods of semi-care carers would not go away overnight in case their mothers had another stroke or a fall: 'I never felt that I could leave her on her own overnight. That might have been exaggerated, but that's how I felt.' Given that this mother was usually capable of getting around and doing many personal care tasks for herself during this period, the carer was undoubtedly being over-cautious, but, as she said, she could not help herself.

During the period of full care both part- and full-time,

respondents were often offered more help, but many worried about the quality and reliability of the care their mothers received at the hands of others. One who was glad to accept the offer of help from a Red Cross volunteer so that she could attend meetings regularly stopped going after coming home on one occasion to find her mother on the floor: 'After that I said no, it's too much, I couldn't go . . . so I didn't go to anything after that.' She added that in any case, going out always seemed to entail extra work when she returned. This was a common theme of those with heavy burdens of care. Most common of all was the dread of coming back to what one termed 'a mopping up operation'. One respondent always looked for the hall light as she came home; if it was on, everything was usually in order. The massive effort required to organize things so that the carer could go out, especially if there was also a family to be considered, was thus compounded by the extra work to be done after the outing. Several respondents said at some point in the interview that they could 'never go out', but this proved to be at odds with their own accounts of their activities. Yet the perception was real enough. In all probability they meant that they found it extremely difficult to get out and under no circumstances could they do anything spontaneously. Two reported finding that even respite care 'wasn't worth it', either because the mother took a long time to settle, or because of the effect of the break on the carer: 'And she came out, and while it did give me a rest one way, in another way it had broken the pattern for me and I didn't really feel I could cope with her much longer and I felt guilty about that.'

Most carers found the incessant routine of caring to have a deadening quality that resulted in feelings of acute claustrophobia – a word frequently used in interviews. The feeling of claustrophobia was not necessarily related to anything specific, such as resentment at missed opportunities, or even forgoing a favourite activity: 'It's not so much that you actually want to go anywhere. It's nice to have the house to yourself. You know, so that you've got your own house – your own territory . . . you're in your own house and you can't be you.' This sort of feeling was particularly strong among the married women respondents and those who did not enjoy mutually supportive relationships with their mothers. The feeling of being trapped or that time was 'ebbing away' was much stronger among carers who lived with dominant or manipulative mothers:

The feeling that you're tied to the situation and you can't get away from it and do anything about it and also you know that it's never going to improve. If you've got the same sort of feelings about a young person or a child ... you know the situation's going to change . . . you know with an older person it's never going to change, it can only get worse.

Not knowing how long caring was likely to continue, especially in cases of chronically ill mothers, was particularly difficult for carers.

Yet caring routines also seem to have developed their own momentum and could prove very hard to break. It was often observed that carers did not use the free time they had to any great personal effect. Several referred to the need to use the odd free afternoon to catch up on household chores, which is understandable if regrettable. One whose mother went to a day centre for a period of four and a half hours a week only once used the time to relax. A very few respondents reported buying in care in order to go out for an afternoon; one used her mother's attendance allowance for this purpose. Many more carers felt that they should not leave their mothers even for short periods, either for fear of what might happen, or in response to the mother's need for their company: 'They don't want anyone else but you.' Where the mother was particularly fearful of being left, the daughter might never take a holiday or even go shopping unaccompanied (see p.66). One respondent used the Crossroads Care Attendant Scheme helper who came in one afternoon a week to help her take her mother out, rather than going out herself.[1] Part of carers' difficulties in taking time for themselves may be traced to the problems in the mother/daughter relationship, but part is also due to their need to keep going. The woman quoted above found that respite care 'broke the pattern' for her and made it more difficult to cope afterwards. Given that many carers feared that they would not be able to 'see it through', this must have been a powerful disincentive to complete relaxation. One carer commented that at first she seized on any opportunity

1 The Crossroads Care Attendant Scheme is a national network of locally organized bodies which provide paid care attendants to give regular, reliable support to physically handicapped people living at home and their relatives. (Briggs and Oliver 1985, pp. 107–11, provide a brief description of this and other nationwide options open to carers.)

for free time to do other things, but 'as time went on you didn't have as much energy'.

We are not of course arguing against the idea of breaks for carers, but merely suggesting that breaks in and of themselves will not necessarily guarantee that carers get adequate relaxation. In other words, the deadening quality of so many caring routines became an end in itself. A downward spiral begins whereby the carer increasingly needs to take a break but has no energy to break out of the routine. Several of our respondents mentioned that they would have welcomed more free time and yet their narratives provided little evidence that they would have used it for themselves. Paradoxically, while enabling some carers to keep going, the routine of caring also made it very difficult for them to know when they had reached breaking point. We referred earlier to the respondent who began to keep a diary because she was not sure how else to determine when she could no longer cope (see p. 41). Again, only when the caring stops either temporarily or permanently does the carer realize the degree of strain that she has been under.

One of the most serious aspects of the constraints placed on carers' time was the way in which many sacrificed not merely outside activities, but also friendships, which in turn rendered the central caring relationship more isolated. 'You couldn't plan to meet people. Most of our friends are scattered over London and you couldn't spare time to meet them. . . . You couldn't say I'm going to drive to the other side of London and spend an evening with friends and then drive back.' Several carers spoke of 'dropping everything' for periods of months or more often years and of trying with more or less success to pick up the threads afterwards. One felt that she had missed seeing a whole generation of younger relatives grow up, another felt particularly guilty because she had stopped seeing a friend who, it later transpired, had been in considerable difficulties and who committed suicide. It is possible to see from some accounts that lack of time was not an insuperable obstacle to sustaining friendships, but rather that unwillingness to leave the mother for whatever reason and a lack of energy were to blame. Respondents were much more likely to keep going to work than to keep up an active circle of friends. In many cases, respondents' jobs consisted of tasks that were relatively routine and which, unlike friendship, did not require much in the way of emotional investment.

The conditions of caring also imposed their own constraints. Very few had sufficiently separate territory of their own to have any privacy for entertaining guests. Five carers talked at length of the embarrassment caused by their mothers' incontinence: 'I mean to say the incontinence . . . because it is very unpleasant . . . she did smell. I knew she couldn't help it. . . . It isn't very easy to have visitors, you know.' A mother with dementia might say odd things, which proved disconcerting for visitors and embarrassing for the carer, who might well not wish others to witness her mother's deterioration. Only two respondents seemed to experience no embarrassment about their mother's condition, one being quite prepared to take her out in her wheel-chair to fêtes and other social events 'all padded up'. Those who managed to keep a reasonably fulfilling social life were usually single women, who had mutually supportive relationships with their mothers *and* a peer group who accepted, and were often also involved in, caring: 'I could take her to a church house group or sometimes a committee meeting . . . she would come and nod off to sleep and make the odd remark. But most of the people I mixed with understood.'

To an outside observer, the majority of respondents led remark-ably restricted lives. Above all, caring imposed a tie and limited their freedom to come and go and in some cases required res-pondents to make hard choices between fulfilling their own and their mothers' needs. The single woman who managed to con-tinue to travel widely, or the married woman who managed to organize regular family outings, was rare. Many carers also had what seemed to be very low expectations: 'Sometimes I would take bits of my holiday to do things I wanted to do, shopping and things like that. Of course we could go for some very nice rides in the car. We considered that was our holiday.' One woman who cared for both her parents full-time from 1945 to 1979 said that when she 'started going about [after her parents died] I realized how much things cost to go places, and what other people expect in their homes, it's given me the shock of my life, it really has'. This woman managed to save money from her mother's small monthly attendance allowance to save for her own funeral, buy carpeting and also have a telephone installed. It must be increasingly unlikely that future generations of women, single or married, will easily accept so little by way of entertainment and creature comforts.

One of the key variables in determining the degree of ease our carers experienced in integrating their caring responsibilities into their lives seems to have been their expectations as to an appropriate lifestyle. These in turn related to peer group expectations and whether caring was regarded as 'natural' or not. Beyond this, the mother's attitude to being cared for, the nature of her relationship with her daughter and the nature of the caring sequence were all crucial in determining the kind of adjustments the carer had to make. The final element making up the complex set of caring relationships is the kind of external supports the daughter could rely on, to which we now turn.

CHAPTER 6

External sources of help

Carers may receive help from kin, friends and neighbours, from voluntary bodies, or from social and health services. In keeping with the new emphasis on supporting the supporters, the sources of help available, particularly in the form of statutory provision, are some of the better researched areas (e.g. Levin, Sinclair, and Gorbach 1983). We focus on the carer's attitude towards and experience of formal and informal help. Just as our view of the nature of the central caring relationship was necessarily refracted through the daughter's gaze, so also is our account of external helping relationships, and without the helper's side of things we cannot verify these accounts. However, potential helpers may find it valuable to see how carers' perceptions of their efforts are linked to other elements that, taken together, comprise the caring experience.

From our exploration in chapter 2 of why respondents cared, to our account in the last chapter of the way in which caring seems to fill all the available gaps in the carer's life, a continuing theme has been the weight of the total responsibility the carer assumes with co-resident care. In this, our findings support those of Wright (1986: 159), who concluded that 'participation by the wider community in the caring process often seemed remarkably sparse'. The idea of a caring network neither captures the reality of the situation nor does the carer expect it to exist. The carer may shoulder primary responsibility for caring willingly or as a matter of last resort. Either way, she may well find herself in need of help, but may have first, a sense of personal inadequacy or embarrassment that prevents her seeking it; second, a fear that her mother would object to outside intervention; third, very rigid ideas herself as to what sorts of help are appropriate (from kin and friends as well as from state services); and finally, may lack knowledge as to what kinds of help she could ask for. Offers of help may in turn be inappropriate if the carer's attitudes and circumstances are not understood.

Just as there may be a substantial gap in understanding between mother and daughter regarding the needs of the other, so there may be a gap between carer and helper, the more so when there is so much to be grasped about the dynamic of the central caring relationship. In these circumstances, a tidy administrative solution to one problem may well serve to exacerbate other problems faced by the carer. An extreme example is that of the respondent who moved into her mother's home to care for her, leaving her husband to visit on weekends. Her GP suggested, quite possibly in exasperation, that both mother and daughter should sell up and move to a new house midway between their current locations. This would have removed the mother from those social supports she had in her home town and would have done nothing to address the central problem of the mother/daughter relationship, which in all probability would have become an even more acute problem for the daughter if she had been faced with performing a balancing act between mother and husband on a daily basis under the same roof. Similarly the offer of practical help in the absence of emotional support may also prove singularly inappropriate in many caring situations. While there is little to be done if a friend or neighbour acts insensitively, it is more incumbent on service providers to be aware of the carer's feelings and concerns.

KIN

It might be expected that carers would look first to kin as a means of support. However, as we observed when considering how the carer came to care, there was often considerable bitterness about the role of kin. Almost half our sample complained about the behaviour of kin. Much more was expected of kin than of friends or neighbours, whose help was seen as a bonus if it was offered.

One respondent reported that her mother had nine brothers and sisters but that they had offered no help at all. She strongly advised other carers to enlist the aid of relatives before assuming the burden of care. Brothers were often criticized for showing a lack of 'proper' concern. A brother in Canada was criticized for never telephoning, others at more accessible distances for never visiting. One respondent very much resented her married sister's lack of involvement: 'In the early days there were a few unpleasant passages when I attempted to talk about sharing, but I gave up that tack and decided there was no mileage in it. . . . I did feel upset about that.' This respondent felt bitter, disapproving and possibly somewhat jealous of her sister. The sister had her mother for holidays each year, but the respondent colluded with her mother in cutting them short because both felt the mother did not get as much attention in the sister's household. Later in the interview, she came back to the issue of her sister's behaviour: 'She didn't come up that often. Well that's not quite fair. It would be once a month. She did come up once a week later, but for very short periods . . . But while I was working she'd never stay the night or anything.' As the burden of care increased for the respondent a friend came to stay and was reported as saying: ' "I don't know how you're still on your feet, I'm going to talk to your sister." What B. said I shall never know. I did say to B.: "Don't say too much, I don't want a family feud", but B. was awfully good and sensible.' After this the sister stayed overnight once a week so that the respondent could get a night's sleep. She was in the house two days before the mother's death: 'The nurse came and thought it was the end but my sister decided not to stay . . . of course I left the decision entirely to her, but of course that was the last night and I was on my own.' This respondent's mother had died some seven years earlier, but she still had a lingering sense of injustice, mingled with the conviction that she and not her sister did the right thing. Little is known in this case of the circumstances of the sister, other than that she had a family of her own. This rather confused expression of bitterness about the sister's perceived lack of involvement, combined with the carer's evident reluctance to allow her mother to stay with her sister for any length of time, illustrates several features in the often conflicting range of emotions felt by a carer. Unless these feelings are appreciated and understood, it is difficult to mediate in an appropriate way. A carer's desire to identify herself as the primary carer may well prove irreconcilable with her need for practical help, because to ask for help threatens her role as primary carer.

Sometimes respondents gave greater acknowledgement to the fact that kin needed to protect themselves from demands they could not meet. One respondent said that her cousin sometimes took her mother for a long weekend, but 'he may have been wary of getting involved with my mother because she was a very demanding person'. Another felt that her brother, who had just remarried, did not want to 'displease' his new wife. On the other hand some instances reveal that despite the respondents' complaint about the behaviour of kin, it is possible that siblings in particular did rather more than they were given credit for. One brother helped financially; another was quite ingenious in constructing various aids to help the mother, but these facts emerged only casually from the respondents' accounts.

It was not so much that respondents expected kin to share the tasks of caring, but rather that they wanted more in the way of emotional support and more feeling that they could share the responsibility for making decisions about what should be done and organizing care:

> I felt . . . that I was getting all the responsibility and my brother was getting away from it. But he was married and had got a family of his own. I mean he used to ring me up and come to see us from time to time, but it wasn't the full responsibility if you know what I mean. But I did feel it was left to me because I was single and I was at home, feeling sorry for myself really.

This statement signals the importance of the central caring relationship. Once a daughter takes on the task of caring, kin also tend to assume that she has taken full responsibility for the mother. Our evidence supports Wilkin's (1979) conclusion that informal supporters provide little help with the daily grind of caring routines. Even in instances where the carer was well-supported, informally and formally, it is more correct to describe her as being 'helped', than the care being 'shared'.

FRIENDS AND NEIGHBOURS

Almost all respondents had some friends and neighbours whom they relied on in very different ways, from the provision of emotional support at a distance to help with intimate personal care tasks. Relationships with friends usually predated the caring period and were based on social contact. As carers became increasingly tied down, so friendships were much harder to sustain. Those friends who kept carers in touch with activities they had once played an active part in were warmly remembered by respondents:

My friends were very good. If anything was happening they'd tell me about it beforehand and they'd come and tell me about it afterwards. I was never left out of things. The folk dancing I had to give up. But they all kept in touch with me. My holiday group – they sent me all the gen about it and sent me cards. I wasn't allowed to feel out of things.

This degree of regular contact sustained on the basis of interests forgone was unusual. The respondent who had moved just before her mother came to stay felt particularly isolated because her friendships could only be maintained by telephone. Those whose friends had slipped away usually made a point of advising other carers not to let this happen. But in fact friendships were only easily maintained with friends who lived locally and only to the degree that the friend could cope with the mother's condition. Several respondents reported their friends to have been 'frightened' by their mothers' deterioration, or that they themselves felt merely that they were unable to continue to see friends who led much more active lives than they were able to do. The mother's own friends, who may play a valuable role in sustaining her morale, also tend to slip away as she deteriorates. In a study evaluating the importance of people in the lives of the elderly, Hawley and Chamley (1986) found that friends scored highest and neighbours lowest on a scale measuring reciprocity, trustworthiness, friendliness, and responsibility. Certainly, two mothers of respondents who had moved some distance in order to live with their daughters, suffered considerable social isolation as a result, which in turn proved an additional strain on the primary carers.

Willmott (1986) has written about the difficulties in differentiating between the role of friend and neighbour and about the importance of recognizing as 'local friends' those who have in previous studies been categorized as neighbours. One of our respondents relied heavily on a neighbour to help with personal care tasks, which was in itself unusual. Indeed the neighbour gave the respondent's mother her last blanket bath before her death. In the course of an intensive two year period of caring it would seem that the relationship became a friendship, but after the mother's death a rupture took place, with the result that the friend has reverted to the 'status' of a neighbour. While the respondent was very reliant on her neighbour as a practical support and confidante while caring, she was referred to as being now too strong willed and interfering. Once the mother's mediating influence was removed, the basis for friendship also disappeared.

On the whole, neighbours tended to give more practical support and friends more in the way of emotional support. This may well be for the reason suggested by Allan (1984): because friendship is often based on sociability and enjoyment, it does not automatically translate into help with caring tasks. Several respondents referred to friends who had said they 'could not have done more'. It was important to carers to receive such legitimation of their work, both from friends and professionals. Friends were also important because they were usually on the carer's side. Thus in situations where the mother was a particularly dominant character, for example, friends could perform the important role of reinforcing the carer's perception that it was her mother rather than herself who was being unreasonable. One commented that her girlfriends were not easily fooled by the charm her mother usually managed to put on for visitors and that they stood by her. Friends whose expectations and lives were very similar to those of the carer were particularly important: 'All my friends are like me, all single, all with mothers.' Friends who 'understood' the lifestyle of the carer from personal experience were extremely valuable. When asked if they had anyone to talk to, many carers commented that they could only talk to someone who had first-hand knowledge of what they were going through. Sometimes old friends did not understand and a hitherto distant office-mate became a confidante, sometimes the carer was completely reliant on professionals for an ear. Friends who were carers were additionally valuable for the information they could provide about services and financial benefits. As Waerness (1984) has commented, an informal network is often the first prerequisite for obtaining support from statutory services. On the whole our respondents seem to have gained more information informally than through formal channels.

Some friends proved important in the help they gave with caring tasks, but to an even greater extent neighbours were relied on in this respect, largely because they were always close at hand. On the whole the kind of help considered appropriate for a neighbour to provide was more closely defined than for a friend.

A local friend might come in and help settle a mother for the night or assist with personal care tasks, as in the case of the respondent who reported that by 'working at it' she and her friend prevented her mother developing bedsores. Those relatively few respondents who were able to have a friend join them in caring for their mothers were also able to discuss their mothers' condition regularly and thus gain a little more distance from caring. Neighbours were very rarely asked to help with personal tasks unless they were nurses. If neighbours performed caring tasks regularly, particularly as sitters, some reciprocity was felt to be very important. Usually the carer left a meal for the sitter. Speaking of an elderly neighbour, who sat with her mother, one said: 'I was giving her a meal as well and knew she was having something to eat and I didn't have to worry [about mother].' Three respondents made the point that, neighbour or friend, the sitter had to be known to the mother. As we have seen, mothers' objections to sitters or domiciliary respite care related to their fears of being left and were exacerbated by an unfamiliar sitter.

As Willmott (1986) has commented, neighbours most commonly practise some form of surveillance. In the case of a mother with dementia who frequently locked herself out, a neighbour would go in the window and let her in: 'One or two people down the street also knew her . . . a fairly busybody type lady would keep an eye. . . . People got to know her actually. People in the shop were quite sympathetic.' Another reported that a neighbour would check on her mother during the day while she was at work: 'He used to come round nearly every day and either call in on some excuse or peer through the window.' As she remarked, there was considerable self-interest involved here because of her mother's dementia: 'Well, you can understand that because . . . neighbours and gas – it was a certain amount of self interest as well, but I was very glad of that.' Above all, perhaps it was the constant presence of sympathetic neighbours that was valued. The neighbour of one respondent rigged up a bell between the two houses so that the respondent's mother could call should there be an emergency while her daughter was out. The reassurance that this sort of help provided was extremely important; this carer did not have to worry so much about what she might find on her return.

CARERS' ATTITUDES TOWARDS HELP

Several carers seem to have done little to seek help, either informal or more especially formal, merely remarking that no help was offered. Sometimes these respondents did not want outside help, either because they genuinely felt they could cope or believed they knew what was best for their mothers, but in a large number of cases other impediments existed to their actively seeking help.

Carers usually set a very high standard for themselves and thus for helpers. The respondent who insisted that care meant more than personal tending, involving talking to the elderly person and helping with her knitting; or the one who felt so guilty because she snapped at her mother: 'You say and do things which are only human really, but *you* don't think you're human, you think I've done that to my own mother or my own father and I'm a dreadful person', were quite typical. Most respondents felt that carers should above all be patient and understanding. Some ten respondents expressed doubts as to whether strangers, even if professionals, could be relied on to 'understand the peculiarities of your mother', whether in respect to diet or aspects of personal care. The injunction to care was experienced so strongly by some respondents that they tended to deny that anyone else *could* care properly for their mothers: 'And I think sometimes you do get to the stage where you think nobody else can do it.' Three respondents felt that as ex-nurses they were genuinely better qualified than anyone else to care for their mothers: 'It was really an extension of what I'd been doing for years.' But others coped alone because they felt that they should do so, whether out of pride and a reluctance to ask for help, or a sense of duty to their mothers. A few made very little mention of help they received and yet their narratives revealed a number of informal helpers and services. In these cases the carer's chief concern was to talk about her (quite genuine) devotion to caring for her mother and in so doing she may have either underestimated, forgotten, or – out of a desire to portray herself first and foremost as a carer – have underplayed the role played by others.

Many more carers wanted help but for one reason or another did not seek it. Three felt that it would have been disloyal to their mothers in some way if they had asked for help. One admitted that she had needed to talk about how she felt:

It would have been more sensible if I'd spoken to a few more people about this 'cos you do tend to think you're a bit of a monster sometimes when you resent and feel badly about having to cope with things like this. And I think that when you get round to talking to folk you realize that most people do feel the same way. . . . I thought for a long time that it was just me being difficult.

However, she did not want to upset her mother. The fact that her mother was mentally alert made it difficult for her to accept help, it was not so much that she did not want any, but rather that she feared making her mother feel that she was a burden. Another said that she had no one to talk to: 'No . . . that's a thing we single women especially, because, er, you feel a bit disloyal, and yet there's times when you'd love to unburden yourself. Because, well, what's going to happen to me?' Yet another expressed very similar feelings and said that she thought it would be easier if there had been a professional to talk to about the problems; she would have felt especially disloyal talking to other kin. These feelings may be compared with the desire, discussed earlier, to hide the mother's dementia or preserve her dignity. Equally strongly represented in the sample was the refusal on the part of mothers to countenance any form of respite care or indeed any stranger coming into the house, even, in two cases, the home help.

Reluctance on the part of the carer to ask for help was widespread. A very few better-off respondents called on informal help from time to time, but preferred to buy in nursing and domestic help. Even those who in the end received various statutory services often said something to the effect that 'you shouldn't ask unless you can't cope', but as we have seen, it was remarkably difficult for carers to decide that they had in fact reached the point where they could no longer cope. Apart from an enormous reluctance to admit their 'failure' to 'see it through', the nature of the caring routines themselves made it difficult for carers to know when they needed a break. The woman who continually refused respite care until the district nurse eventually intervened and insisted on it, was a case in point. As the respondent described it, she became so drained by the caring routine that she could no longer take any decisions. By the end this was undoubtedly true, but this respondent was also very anxious to please her mother and to undertake caring for her herself. She would have felt a personal failure if she had asked for help earlier. Two respondents seemed to think that if they asked for help they would be demonstrating their unsuitability as carers and the mother would be institutionalized: 'If you explain you want a lot of things *done*, of course, you're a nuisance to people and they think, I'll put them in a geriatric ward.' This respondent, who cared for her mother with her sister, felt very guilty that they both went to work all day and left their mother on her own. Their fears may be analogous to those of parents worrying that social workers will take their children into care. Certainly they tried hard not to make themselves conspicuous to the authorities.

Much more common was the statement: 'I didn't feel I could ask', which often stemmed partly from the carer's sense of guilt and personal inadequacy (Levin, Sinclair, and Gorbach 1983, found this to be a major cause of carers' reluctance to seek help), and partly from the mother's reluctance to be cared for by others: 'this sort of guilt feeling, as if you're trying to palm your mother off on to somebody else, you know'. This respondent added: 'You're very much on your own, there's no, um, I didn't really know where to go I suppose. I would now but I didn't at the time.' Lack of information and knowledge about voluntary organizations and statutory services was one of the strongest themes running through the comments on sources of help and something that remained a bitter legacy in the minds of many:

We did get a commode only after I'd had a locum doctor in . . . it was a lady doctor and she said, 'Haven't you got a commode? Haven't you got a bath seat?' . . . and that's what started that off. But her [mother's] own doctor never told her anything. She thought the sun rose and set around him, but er he never told me anything I could give her or anything I could get for her. It wasn't until somebody had told me and said to me, 'Well, if you must go away for a holiday they can put her in a home for a fortnight, and they can do it every year' and it was the same friend that had told me everything else. And when I spoke to the doctor, 'Oh yes, of course'. I didn't say it, but I felt like saying, 'Why didn't you say something or didn't you think I'd ask?' But I felt that if you don't know these things you're not going to get the help you should have. Because the help's there, around, but why should you have to shop around for it?

These comments bespeak a pride in coping and a deferential attitude towards the medical profession, as well as a belief that you should not have to ask for help.

Respondents' feelings about the help they did or did not receive tended to be much more straightforwardly positive or negative than about other aspects of caring. The majority felt that, for whatever reason, they were doing the best they could for their mothers, that they were at times under considerable strain and that their problems should have been recognized by a professional worker. One said: 'It's not easy to fight [for services] when you're always so tired'; furthermore, carers felt a deep-seated sense of injustice that they should have had to battle for help at all. It may not be realistic to expect professional workers to divine a carer's needs, but the comments from our interviews indicate that careful and sensitive probing is usually needed to encourage the carer to reveal her true circumstances.

FORMAL HELP

Thus to establish a carer's needs is in all likelihood a delicate problem. To put it another way, the language of supply and demand in relation to carers and caring is rarely explicit or measurable in any straightforward fashion. For example, it is doubtless true, as Levin, Sinclair, and Gorbach (1983) suggest, that carers require more help in respect to bathing the elderly and infirm, but if the carer feels the bathing attendant violates her elderly relative's sense of due proprieties the help will be rejected. Recent analysis of General Household Survey data has suggested that there are significant limits to how far formal services can substitute for home care in matters of personal tending (Evandrou *et al*. 1986). The nature of the help offered, practical and/or emotional, together with the way in which it is offered, is crucial in securing an effective outcome, viz., supporting the carer. The vast majority of carers want to care, but given the kinds of strain they are likely to experience are right to expect help. The bitterness expressed about service provision was greater than that expressed about the lack of support from kin. Not only did expectations of support often remain at least partially unfulfilled, but carers felt considerable resentment at having to make so much effort to obtain services.

The array of services provided via health and social services

departments is bewildering and the most consistent themes in
the accounts of respondents were: first, the lack of information
they had as to what was available; second, the variability in services (those who had moved from one area to another were often
astonished by this); and third, the considerable number of over-
laps and gaps in provision. One carer who was about to assume
responsibility for caring for another relative remarked: 'Having
done all this with mother it doesn't worry me because I know
where to go.' Not knowing 'where to go' is one of the most worrying and frustrating aspects of caring. One respondent who did
not have a telephone reported writing a constant stream of letters
to a variety of places asking for help. Her request for a bath rail
first made in 1978 (possibly to the wrong department) was met in
1984, shortly after her mother entered a home. Seven respondents were not told anything about the attendance allowance; one
eventually found out about it from her solicitor (she had been
visited by a health visitor and social worker), and another from
the National Council for Carers and their Elderly Dependants.
Despite the preponderance of middle-class women in our sample,
who were for the most part both well-educated and articulate,
most had little expertise in seeking help from government agencies. One respondent, who was still extremely angry about the
lack of help she received from statutory services, said the social
worker who called every time her mother was about to go into a
local authority home (see Appendix D) for respite care never
asked about how she was managing or told her about the provision of incontinence pads or the attendance allowance. All he did
was fill out the form regarding her mother's finances: 'What did
they think was going to happen to her income since they'd done
the last one? . . . Nice tidy house, nice capable lady, so you don't
have to do anything.' Because many respondents were reluctant
for one reason or another to ask for help, they often did without
until goaded by necessity into making more determined demands.
One reported that she found it extremely difficult to make anything
but a polite and hesitant request for aid, but was eventually forced
to 'storm the citadel' in an effort to get nursing help. Two others
spoke of gradually learning 'to stand up for themselves'. An
interesting reflection of the way in which carers assumed the full
responsibility for the care of their mothers is the way in which all,
including the married women, appear to have also shouldered the
burden of dealing with the various service providers.

The first port of call for most carers in seeking advice and help tended to be their GP and, on the whole, GPs received the worst press from our carers' accounts. Of the eight respondents who commended their work, five added that they were 'lady doctors' and seemed to think that, as in the case of female employers, a woman doctor was more likely to have an understanding of the problem:

> The two men, I could do without them because their attitude was one of them, 'Well, hard luck, that's your problem', and the other one just said, 'Well, we've all got to come to it and it comes to some in different ways than others.' I just waited until I knew I could get the lady doctor.

The majority were, to say the least, sceptical of what their GPs offered. In particular, none of the carers whose mothers developed dementia received any information from GPs. Even when the GP was described as 'sympathetic', he was also said to lack either useful information or time. One reported that: 'I never actually got anywhere through the doctor. I mean the doctor just used to look at me with a long face and say, "Ah yes, it will be difficult" [laugh].' And: 'Doctors just come in for a few minutes and they're gone', or: 'Doctors don't know... they don't think ... and they're *busy*.' Respondents felt frustrated that GPs seemed not to appreciate the problems because they were unable to take the time to observe them and seemed to have little in the way of any intuitive understanding.

One GP was convinced that the mother should be institutionalized but the daughter wanted more domiciliary nursing help. The respondent reported more than once in the course of the interview that:

> I used to ask him . . . I said I'll pay for a nurse and he said no, 'Even if we do give you a nurse or a day help your mother would still have to cope with the stairs . . . you'd hate one day to come home and find your mother with a broken leg at the bottom of the stairs.'

This GP offered no appropriate services to a respondent who wanted to carry on looking after her mother and merely succeeded in inducing guilt. Another respondent complained about:

the number of medical people who when you say you've got problems say 'well, if you want to get out dear, she's got the commode, leave her a plate of sandwiches and off you go.' I had that several times. I really don't think the medical profession have come to terms with the problem. No way have they come to terms with the problem – maybe they're just trained to do the medical bit. . . . I don't know what's happened in their home life, whether they have ever actually had the experience and know what it's like to juggle with a commitment to a job and three meals a day and someone's diabetic or incontinent and needs you and can't get out and can't be left and all this sort of thing – they have no idea how it all comes out – and would they in fact if it were their mother, would they leave their mother all day alone in a house knowing that she's a bit wobbly on her pins and just give her a flask and a plate of sandwiches and nip off for the day with peace of mind? Would they do that? It's very easy to say you will. And after all if someone is quite elderly they can't always cope very well with trays and flasks. . . .

Again the overwhelming sense here is of a lack of appreciation on the part of the medical profession of the meaning of caring and of the circumstances of carers. This woman's doctor took the view that married women who worked did so for pin money and advised that she could best alleviate her burdens by giving up work, ignoring the fact that her income was crucial for paying the mortgage. Other respondents reported that professional helpers assumed that they would be available to give all their time to caring, ignoring their roles in the wider society, whether as workers or mother and ignoring their need for a measure of self-fulfilment.

Nor did GPs always appreciate that in an intense caring relationship medical advice could end up assuming greater significance than had perhaps been intended:

The only thing I remember him saying was that she might die tomorrow or she might go on for years. Now what do you make of that? And so to begin with, bearing in mind the tomorrow business made me more afraid than ever of leaving her.

This respondent took the idea that her mother might die tomorrow literally, with the result that she experienced greater stress. Very few respondents seem to have received prompt and comprehensive advice from their GPs as to the range of services available; indeed one respondent reported that she was now actively involved in a local voluntary group trying to put such information into local doctors' surgeries. A significant number received only a bare minimum of help from GPs and district nurses, together with a variety of services from health visitors, home helps, social workers, day centres and institutions taking their mothers for respite care. In several instances the type of help offered was by no means appropriate. Two respondents said they could have coped with the caring task themselves and indeed wished to do so – what they really wanted was more financial help rather than services. Two others wanted more domiciliary nursing at home rather than the respite care offered in one case, and the social work and home help services received in the other.

Nor was there any overwhelming consensus that one service was more appreciated than another. Those praising district nurses stressed that they were appreciated above all because they provided practical help, 'body help', as one respondent called it. Many respondents both feared and resented having to do basic nursing tasks and therefore valued the nurse's visits. On the whole older nurses were preferred to younger ones, largely because they were perceived to have more experience and a more general appreciation of the habits of elderly people and the meaning of caring. One young district nurse was reported to have had no knowledge of the mysteries of elderly people's underwear, with disastrous effects: 'I wish somebody would teach them how to put old people's clothes on. Because I came home one day when they had dressed her . . . and she said she couldn't to go the toilet all day because they had put her suspender belt over her knickers.' Similarly health visitors and home helps were described as 'saviours' by some, but were criticized by others. One health visitor gained for a respondent's mother access to a day centre which proved extremely responsive to the mother's needs and was described by the respondent as a 'marvellous place. If only there were places like that to have them 24 hours a day.' Another gained access to a day centre through a social worker. However the hours of day centres were often awkward and rarely fitted in even with part-time work hours. Most of the thirteen respondents whose mothers attended ended up having to chauffeur their mothers because they were not on the ambulance route or because the timing of transport was highly inconvenient for the daughter's work routine. Paradoxically, as the condition of the person cared for worsened, supports such as day centres were often withdrawn, because staff could no longer cope with the needs of the elderly person.

Apart from problems of access to services and the mixed views held by respondents as to the utility of various services, the most common concern running through the narratives was that of reliability of services. One remembered becoming anxious in case the new supply of incontinence pads was late arriving, another complained that she could never count on the district nurse to arrive in time to help get her mother up or put her to bed, and another that her mother hated sitting in her dressing-gown, sometimes for hours, waiting for the bathing attendant to arrive. Two respondents complained that the meals on wheels service was sometimes very late so that they felt obliged to leave their mothers a snack in case they got hungry or did not like the food when it arrived. 'You never knew when they were coming' runs as a constant refrain through the interviews, and any service that respondents could count on was much more likely to be appreciated. Two respondents who had Crossroads Care Attendants commented very favourably on how they arrived at a fixed time, allowing the respondents to plan their days. 'That was really what we found most helpful because you know they come at a *certain time* and they take over . . . [her emphasis].' For many carers the routines associated with caring were finely timed and finely balanced with other responsibilities. And for elderly women too, routine was very important. An absence of reliable services increased tension for both parties, devaluing the work of the carer by assuming she could adjust to times chosen by the service providers, and degrading the elderly person who was often expected to wait in her dressing-gown, sometimes for hours at a time. As a result, carers often resorted to performing the task themselves.

Provision of appropriate and sympathetic help could be the make or break factors for carers. In the case of an unmarried respondent, whose mother required full care from 1976 when she had a stroke until she died in 1981, no help was forthcoming from kin. Friends were assiduous in keeping in touch, but the respondent relied on various health and social services for help when she suddenly had to deal with an incontinent and immobile mother.

The GP played a crucial role in contacting the district nurse, who immediately organized the provision of incontinence pads and one-way sheets, and a physiotherapist. The respondent also received a hoist, ripple bed and chair, wheelchair and ramp into the garden, commode and laundry service. Her only complaint concerned the bathing service, which she felt did not show due regard for her mother's sense of modesty. 'I had such help . . . I didn't know what I was entitled to, what I could expect. I was very, very fortunate.' The GP also gave her a phone number for use day or night and she used it the day her mother was dying to contact the nurse.

In contrast, two cases in particular illustrate the way in which overlap between services, inappropriate help, and gaps in service provision could combine to make the carer's position well-nigh intolerable. In the first case, a divorced respondent with four children cared full-time for a mother with Parkinson's disease and dementia over a period of three years. Her GP would come and visit, but the respondent described his visits as extremely brief and said that she did not feel that he understood what it was like for her. A social worker was described as a 'dead loss' because he thought her mother looked well and answered his questions properly; in fact the mother was able to answer 'yes' or 'no', but had little or no understanding of what was being said to her. The social worker also offered the respondent a home help, whom she did not want, wanting rather to have her mother out of the house on a regular basis for a few hours so that she could have the house to herself.

A geriatrician assessed the mother and said she should go to a day centre:

> It gave me a break for four or five hours during the day, but you were here in the morning waiting for the ambulance, not knowing what time it was coming at, having her ready at half nine, it might not come until eleven, and you had to be here at half three waiting for it to come back, it mightn't come until five.

The geriatrician also ordered a course of injections which produced a bad reaction. He then handed the mother over to a psychiatrist, who disagreed with the medication that had been ordered: 'Between them they messed up the injections.' By this time the mother was getting violent and the respondent felt 'drained'. At this point the district nurse started to call every morning to help get the mother up and after four weeks insisted on respite care. This respondent felt she was 'saved' in the end by the district nurse who had been the only one to recognize the strain she was under.

In the second case, the respondent was married without children. Her mother was diabetic and suffered a stroke in 1973 which meant that she could no longer perform personal care tasks. She became incontinent in 1974, suffered kidney failure in 1977, was hospitalized for a time in 1982, and from then until she died in 1984 required constant care from the respondent. The GP rushed in and rushed out:

> It was as though I didn't exist. . . . It was very much the attitude of, if you cannot cope, let me know, I will make arrangements. I do remember having one stand-up row with him . . . she's not a parcel of rubbish to be sent off. No one ever asked me how I was coping.

The last sentence of this quotation provides the key to many of this respondent's problems with services. Neither the GP, district nurse, nor social worker seem to have taken the time to check that this respondent had information on matters such as aids and incontinence pads and financial assistance.

The district nurse called from 1973 to give injections for pernicious anaemia and then insulin injections. She apparently asked the respondent to give these, which she eventually did, but disliked having to do it. The times of the day centre were too awkward for her mother to attend regularly. Until the last two years her mother went away for two weeks respite care in the summer, which the respondent found out about by seeing an advertisement in the paper and telephoning the Social Services Department. After about two years her mother went for an additional week at Easter: 'I was never really given any indication of how much time you could have.' During the last fifteen months her mother was assessed for an appropriate form of institutional care, but the authorities were unable to decide whether she should enter a local authority old people's home or a geriatric hospital (see Appendix D): 'She finally ended up for two weeks in a home which was dreadful, and landed back in hospital with me saying no way does she go back there.' A second geriatric consultant deemed that she should go back to a local authority home, but the social worker refused: 'Eventually she went to the geriatric hospital and I went down there and had one look around and took her back home and that was it. She stayed home until the last week when she was ill and she died in hospital.' Two aspects of this particularly stressful experience stand out; first, the way in which, while the amount of help increased as the mother's condition deteriorated rapidly during the last fifteen months, the process of assessment for and admission to an institution was very badly handled, and second, the lack of any emotional support for the carer throughout the period of care.

Several other respondents complained about the inadequacy of assessment procedures, especially for admission to institutional care, but also for day care places. A respondent who very much wanted to care for her mother who was developing dementia, described the following experience:

He [the social worker] kept saying to me, 'You've had your mother long enough. You've got to let go now. Why don't you put her in a home?' And I said, 'Look, I don't want to put her in a home. It was my father's wish that she should die with me; all I want is someone to give me a hand, just sort of come in in the morning, like a daily help. . . . ' [The social worker] kept saying, 'Oh, just like your children one day have to go, you have to let your mother go.' And he decided they would take her into hospital . . . for assessment. . . . That was such a terrible experience. She went in there, she was walking perfectly

When the daughter visited her mother a few days later:

We could have died [tears]. My mother was sitting there soaking wet, she was obviously drugged, half asleep . . . we spent ten minutes trying to get her to wake up. I know when somebody's drugged and when they're sleeping . . . she just sat there with her tongue hanging out. . . . I said I'm not moving from here 'til I see a doctor . . . in the end he admitted she was drugged, which he said was part of the way of treating a person. I don't know. I still don't know.

After this the respondent reported that her mother became increasingly incontinent and was admitted to an old people's home for day care: 'They they started to put her in a room by herself because she was too noisy and repeating herself.' By this point in the narrative, it is hard to decide how far the respondent was able to distinguish between the effects of services and the effects of her mother's progressive deterioration. But it is clear that with greater communication on the part of the professionals involved and more emotional support she would have found the procedures less threatening and may have been able to cope better with the changes in her mother. As it was, she felt the biggest mistake she had made was in letting her mother go to the hospital for assessment.

Emotional support for the carer is crucial. Carers need support in order to face the problems they experience in caring and to reinforce their own self image. As one put it: 'What I always felt I missed was someone who particularly cared for me.' Many carers reported that friends had reassured them that they could not have done more, similarly the legitimation provided by professionals for their efforts was important. One respondent who felt that she should have sought further specialist advice during her mother's final illness would have suffered far less guilt had someone taken the time to reassure her. The respondent who already felt guilty about putting her mother in respite care was upset further by a receptionist's rudeness. Fairly common anxieties about what would happen if the carer herself fell sick could easily have been dealt with by more sympathetic support. One respondent remarked that carers needed someone to tell them not only what sort of help they could get, but that they should 'expect to feel guilty'. A carer who had been a nurse was assumed by the geriatrician to be able to cope with all eventualities, but nevertheless felt she could have done with a bit more 'moral support' (a similar point is made by Davey 1984). When one carer asked to talk to her GP about how she was feeling, she was simply rebuffed:

> The GP came in and said, 'You want to talk to me?' So I started off and I suppose you don't know which bit to start with and I suppose it's difficult, so I don't know, I suppose I started off with something about the difficulty of the toiletting and everything and he looked up and said, 'I haven't got time to sit here and listen to your emotional problems' and walked out.

Supporting the carer necessarily involved professionals in offering emotional as well as practical help, first because some carers feel that they cannot talk about their problems in caring unless in confidence (see p.97) and second, because emotional support involves a degree of sympathetic communication during which it is likely that the helper will learn much more of the carer's circumstances and needs. When asked about what they would have liked by way of support a large number of respondents mentioned some form of back-up to give them the feeling that there was someone they could contact: 'Someone at the end of a telephone', or 'someone you wouldn't be a nuisance to', as two respondents put it, reflecting the strong feeling that the first need was to talk the problem through.

One of the most important points at which carers need emotional support is when they are facing the institutionalization or the death of the elderly person. For the thirteen respondents who made a conscious decision to admit their mothers to institutional care and the further seven whose mothers became so ill that hospitalization was necessary, the end of co-resident care usually proved traumatic. Of the thirteen, six were single and seven married carers. None wished to admit her mother to an institution, indeed in two cases it was a husband and brother respectively who insisted on the move. Deimling and Poulshock's (1985) research has shown that the attitude of caregivers towards institutional care is at least as important a variable in the decision to admit an elderly person to an institution as the physical and emotional health of the person cared for, or the degree of stress experienced by the carer. In the case of carers who, like the majority of our respondents, have committed themselves to caring for a relative 'to the end', the decision to seek admission to an institution is inevitably problematic and it may be that the carer finds it very difficult to decide that she can no longer cope. This explains why the decision to seek institutional care was taken by a husband and brother in two cases. In three others, the carer attempted to find a place in a home for her mother, but then drew back, either because the carer considered the institution unsatisfactory, or because the mother voiced dissatisfaction. Even in one case where the daughter was able to discuss the decision with her mother who was physically frail but mentally alert, and who was by no means averse to going into institutional care, the daughter felt ultimately responsible, and guilty, for taking the decision.

Most of these carers were neither able nor willing to stop caring overnight. Hospital and nursing home staff, however, often tended to assume that their role was ended. One respondent, whose mother was still alive at the time of the interview and living in an old people's home where she had been for two years, still felt profoundly ambivalent about her being there: 'I think it was far harder to adjust to her going [than to care for her]. It was the hardest thing, much like bereavement. I said to her, "If I had known it would be like this I wouldn't have let you go." ' She continues to visit her mother two or three times a week: 'You have the travel time and the time you spend with her and any little commissions she wants done, which takes a lot of the week.' In other words, even though her mother is now in a home the daughter continues to care; indeed when the elderly person enters an institution the carer effectively reverts to a period of semi-care. Her mother has settled in well at the home and has begun to play an active role in its communal life, while the daughter finds herself without the companionship that was the reward for caring. Nevertheless, in many respects she is fortunate in that the staff in the home welcome her visits and allow her to continue to undertake personal care tasks for her mother, such as bathing and hair washing. Most respondents reported that they were not allowed to perform any personal care tasks for their mother and some felt they were not even especially welcome as visitors: 'I'm not supposed to have any worries now. She's in there, they are looking after her, that's their attitude.' American institutional practices seem to be more receptive to carers who continue to provide elements of personal care, although more out of a regard for the elderly person's welfare than out of an understanding of the carer's position (Hooyman and Lustbader 1986: 285–305).

It is impossible for carers to end the caring relationship overnight. Most felt very guilty for in the end doing what they had initially rejected and putting their mothers in a home or hospital, and these feelings were compounded when they were denied the opportunity of continuing to care. One respondent decided that her mother, who had dementia, would have to enter a home, but when they arrived her mother announced that she would not stay, using whole sentences in a manner she had not done for months. Eventually, the mother was admitted to a psychiatric hospital. The ambulance failed to arrive to collect her and so the respondent drove her, arriving at lunchtime when there was no one available to talk to her about her mother's admission:

I was in a numb state really. . . . There is a lot of guilt. The sort of sentence, 'How can you let your mother go to a place like that?' hangs in the air. Well I would never let my mother go to a place like that. . . . I felt that a lot to begin with. At the moment I can't see what alternative there is. I could have given up work, but I would have had to move . . . it would have been such an upheaval and I don't think I would have been any good at it. I was stretching myself really. . . . The first year there I found quite difficult . . . the first 15–20 minutes of every visit I used to spend in tears . . . there are certain things you have to get used to, like the clothes, they won't let them have any of their own clothes. And whereas I always kept Mum's hair permed [tears] it just always has to be kept short and straight.

Another respondent who had a nervous breakdown after her mother died found the period her mother spent in a home very traumatic:

I couldn't switch off. I used to go and see her more or less every day. When she first went in she was quite bright, but they said 'We'd much rather you didn't come in every day because you're going to upset her.' I could see she was deteriorating so I just had to go and see her.

This respondent also felt that the staff did not look after her mother as well as she had. Her mother developed a rash from incontinence and the staff also insisted that she wear her false teeth even though they did not fit properly. When the respondent visited, she took the teeth out, but the staff insisted that her mother should keep them in: 'I thought they knew best, but she was uncomfortable with them. I thought they should be out.' However, she did not feel able to talk to the staff about her mother's care. While it is common knowledge that people often find fault with the treatment given their loved ones because they are displacing their anger or grief that the person is ill or dying, it is nevertheless very difficult and in fact unnecessary for the erstwhile carer to be so totally displaced. The carer cannot and does not stop caring because the elderly person enters an institution.

Emotional support for relatives of the dying has attracted considerable attention particularly from those involved in the hospice movement. As Taylor (1983: 54) has observed:

Gerontologists tend to be wary of placing too much emphasis

on the care of the dying in respect of health provision for the elderly, and prefer to stress the positive opportunities, given appropriate support, for elderly people to retain maximum independence and quality of life. The danger in this is that it ignores the fact of approaching death and that the achievement of a 'good death' may be extremely valued – and may only be achieved if both patient and carer are prepared for it.

In two cases carers reported that doctors refused to face the fact that their mothers were dying. In one of these a clergyman helped by visiting and making it easy for the mother to talk as if she was dying. Insufficient preparation for the old person's death and lack of any counselling afterwards (which was the usual experience) prolonged the difficult period of adjustment for the carer. One respondent who had a complete breakdown after her mother's death received no professional support and, from friends, only advice that she could not cope with, such as the idea that she ought to think of selling her house. Five carers reported their only source of emotional support to have been voluntary societies such as the Alzheimer's Disease Society, MIND, the NCCED and the Association of Carers. Ironically, only two carers we interviewed could afford the time to attend the meetings of such societies while caring, but telephone conversations and newsletters provided the reassurance above all that there were others similarly or worse placed, with comparable problems and anxieties.

The plight of a full-time carer who may be caring for a mother with dementia, whose relationship with her mother may be problematic, whose mother may not co-operate in her care and who may have little practical or emotional support from either kin or friends, is severe. In this sort of situation the carer is entirely dependent on outside formal or voluntary help. Such an extreme situation is rare, but professional help can in any event prove crucial in *enabling* the carer to care. For help from statutory services to be 'enabling' it must be 'appropriate' and it must be available before the carer starts to suffer extreme stress; one carer received help only after she collapsed mentally, another only after she had severely strained herself physically. And for help to be 'appropriate', helpers must both listen to carers and make a judicious assessment of all aspects of the carer's circumstances.

Koshberg and Cairl (1986) have devised a 'Cost of Care Index' to assist in the process of assessment. Comprising twenty items, it probes elements of carer well-being, both emotional and material, and the carer's perceptions of her relationship with the person cared for and with significant others. Such an instrument may well provide a useful point of departure, although used by itself it would be too blunt to penetrate some of the more common dilemmas uncovered by our interviews. For example, a carer insisting that she can cope may genuinely be able to do so, or she may not wish to admit that she needs help, or she may have reached breaking point without realizing it. Sensitive professional assessment may be particularly crucial if the elderly person is dominant in the household. As one respondent put it: 'I'd have liked someone to persuade her to go into a home occasionally so I'd have a holiday occasionally.' The views of the person cared for may crucially affect the kind of help that carers will consider appropriate. Helpers who confine their assessment to a strict appraisal of the needs of the carers (for rest, perhaps) and of the person cared for (for aids or medication), and ignore the quality and nature of the primary caring relationship, risk the rejection of their offers of assistance.

In many cases, what is required may be solely offers of practical help – such as a good laundry service to relieve the opprobrium of incontinence. We would argue, however, that an additional element of support is required: an expressed appreciation of the situation of the carer and person cared for, and expressed recognition of the valuable work of caring. In order to achieve this, supporters of the supporters must look to the wider circumstances of the carer than purely practical issues. It may be that this role should not be the exclusive province of professionals. We have already seen how supportive existing carers' groups can be in offering mutual support and advising about 'where to go'. These groups are widely scattered, and access to them is not easy for hard-pressed carers who cannot leave their homes without elaborate arrangements. Investment in an infrastructure of support groups for supporters, plus consideration of how access could be widened – for instance through telephone counselling – could go far to constructing the support network for carers, which is so often discussed but so rarely found to exist in practice. Certainly, a majority of carers expressed a desire to know that there was someone they could contact. In their study of support for the mentally handicapped, Ayer and Alaszewski (1984) recommended the development of contact points within the statutory services. Whether developed on a voluntary or statutory basis, such a development seems highly desirable.

Informal care for the elderly is often lauded because it is flexible. By this it is usually meant that it is more responsive to the elderly person's needs. This may be true, but the caring routines that must be established by an informal carer are often remarkably inflexible. If service providers are to intervene adequately to support these individualized and inflexible routines, it is they who must demonstrate the greatest flexibility of all. Indeed when respondents were asked what they would have liked by way of support there was no uniformity in their replies. They differed dramatically in terms of how far and in what ways they wanted to 'share the care'. Five felt care should be confined to the family and expressed a desire only for more financial aid: 'What one needs is people who share one's care . . . and feelings for the parent . . . and then you don't have to explain everything, you know that they'd care for them as you would.' A rather larger number felt very strongly that there should be greater formal provision. The most-often mentioned preference was for more respite care (which accords with the findings of Levin, Sinclair, and Gorbach 1983), but some wanted this to take the form of regular institutional care provided every few weeks or every few months, while some wanted domiciliary care overnight or for a couple of hours each day. This variability is important because as Glendinning (1983) observed in her study of parents caring for disabled children, support for supporters is discussed all too often in terms of the provisions of alternatives: either services or cash, either domiciliary or residential care. Different carers need different kinds and combinations of help.

Fear has often been expressed that state support for informal carers will result in formalizing the informal. This is only likely to be the case if by their inflexibility statutory services dragoon carers into frameworks not of their own choosing. But it must be recognized that effective support of each and every carer requires careful assessment and understanding, and must necessarily be a highly individualized and more costly business.

CHAPTER 7

Responses to caring

By drawing together the various aspects of caring discussed so far, we may differentiate three broad sets of responses by which women sought to fit caring into their everyday lives – 'coping' responses. Our delineation of these is tentative and we would not wish to suggest that they are entirely mutually exclusive, or that they provide an exhaustive analysis of responses to caring, or that they illustrate all the issues discussed thus far. However, they were the most prevalent responses in our sample and in discussing them we may also show how the themes we have focused on so far fit together in the everyday lives of our respondents.

We chose three terms to represent these responses: 'balancing act', 'integration', and 'immersion'. Seventeen respondents performed something of a balancing act between caring for their mothers and caring for house and family and/or going out to work; fourteen, almost all single, managed to integrate caring into their lives; and a further ten tended to immerse themselves in caring to the exclusion of all outside interests. Again the majority of these women were single, although three married women were also judged to give caring priority over home and family. Those performing a balancing act between caring and other priorities tended to experience caring as stressful, while for those who experienced caring as an integral part of their lives, it served to 'fill the gaps' – to give a purpose to their lives – rather than to exert conflicting demands. Those immersing themselves in their mothers' care did so for a variety of reasons. In cases where this response followed from the mother's dominant personality, the carer was likely to experience growing isolation and in one case this clearly resulted in the collapse of the carer at the death of the mother, the void proving too large to fill. However, in other cases, as with some of those who managed to integrate caring into their lives, carers immersed themselves in the caring task because they felt it was supremely worthwhile and because they saw it as a challenge. Thus none of these responses should be categorized as wholly positive or negative. Indeed, the advantage of our overview of the caring process is that we see how positive and negative factors interweave throughout.

Responses to caring must be related to the way in which daughters came to care; the nature of the caring task; the relationship between mother and daughter and whether the daughter co-operated in her care; the importance the daughter attached to other activities and the nature of her lifestyle; and to the amount of help she received (see Table 7.1).

In three cases we had difficulty in deciding whether the respondent was an 'immerser' or 'balancer'. These were cases in which the respondents experienced the pull of work or family throughout the caring period, but who nevertheless identified firmly with their role of carer and sought as far as possible to immerse themselves in it. In the end, we identified these women as balancers, because their priority was to balance caring with paid work. In one case the carer's paid work ended at almost the same time as caring, and she, not surprisingly, suffered a breakdown.

A majority of those women who strove to achieve a balance between caring and other activities and responsibilities were married and had taken a conscious decision to live with their mothers. These women experienced enormous tension as a result of their efforts to balance caring with their family responsibilities and to prevent caring intruding on their family routine. Furthermore, a significant minority of balancers received no support from either kin or professionals. Single women balancers were more likely to be determined to maintain their work identities. They engaged in a 'mad scramble' all week to fit everything in and also often experienced considerable guilt about leaving their mothers; however they seem to have had rather more support than the married women in this category from external sources, especially from kin and friends.

Most 'balancers' felt a strong obligation to care and considerable affection for their mothers, notwithstanding the fact that of the seventeen, fourteen experienced a problematic relationship

Table 7.1 *Responses to caring: integrators, balancers, and immersers*

	integrators	balancers	immersers
Marital status			
Single	13	8	7
Married	1	7	3
Divorced	–	2	–
Support			
Kin ⎫ mutually	4	4	6
Professional ⎬ exclusive	3	5	–
Kin & professional	6	1	1
None	1	7	4
Mother's illness			
Physical	11	6	3
Mental	2	7	4
Physical & mental	1	4	3
Mother co-operates in care	10	9	4
Mother/daughter relationship during caring			
Good	9	3	1
Bad	2	10	5
Good to bad	3	4	4
Relative importance of work or caring			
Caring more important	9	5	4
Work more important	1	8	1
Caring & work equally important	3	1	1
Not in paid employment during caring period	1	3	4

with their mothers and about half had mothers who did not co-operate in their care. Many also believed that caring was extremely important and should be undertaken: 'You can always get another job, you can't get another Mum can you?' On the other hand, they also wanted to maintain an identity outside caring. For the small minority who felt little affection and a fierce attachment to their careers, the only rationale for taking on the responsibility of caring was derived from the satisfaction of knowing they had done 'the right thing'. A majority of 'balancers' felt that their jobs were a more important source of identity than caring, hence their struggle to balance caring and paid work. One woman who initially attempted to balance caring for her mother with caring for her husband *and* working full-time commented that it would have been easier to 'think of myself as a carer right from the beginning'. However, those who followed this course and immersed themselves in caring tended to experience more trouble in adjusting to the end of co-resident caring. It is important to recognize that 'thinking of yourself as a carer' may make it easier to ask for help as a carer, and to acknowledge the strains which may arise, but should not necessarily mean that the carer is forced to eschew all other activities and identify herself solely with caring. Balancers at least tended to have a 'normal' life to return to after caring ended, whereas integrators and immersers experienced considerably greater problems in adjusting.

The five balancers who said that they felt caring to be more important to them than work were all married women who were struggling more to balance the demands of their mothers with those of their husbands and children. In the end, the vast majority of the married women respondents felt that they had to put the needs of husbands and children first, although the decision to admit the mother to hospital was usually extremely traumatic.

Those who managed to 'integrate' caring into their lives were women who were, with one exception, single and who had lived with their mothers for most of their adult lives. Furthermore, several regarded caring as 'natural' while most of the rest drifted into it without consideration of the consequences. In most of these cases kin were supportive, and over half received some support from professionals through the caring period. Unlike the mothers of those balancing care, or immersing themselves in it, their mothers tended to suffer more from physical than mental illness. In most cases the mother/daughter relationship was mutually supportive and caring was accompanied by a deep degree of companionship, with the mothers co-operating in their care. Indeed the label we have given this category of responses suggests a positive and satisfying caring experience. However in a minority of cases, while caring filled the gaps in the carer's life, the central caring relationship was not companionate; this was certainly true in one case where the mother suffered from dementia and in another where she was essentially uncooperative. These two carers responded to a deeply felt injunction to care, but received little appreciation from their mothers, which for others was what made the experience additionally satisfying and worthwhile.

The ten carers who 'immersed' themselves in caring had for the most part begun by trying to integrate caring into their lives, but found that it took over, with the result that these respondents gave up their jobs and usually most of their social lives. Some, like some balancers and integrators, treated the new situation as a challenge, approaching the organization of a caring routine as they had their office work, exercising their ingenuity in seeking solutions to the problems of their mothers' incontinence or immobility. And some were additionally happy to do this because they felt that caring was the most worthwhile thing they could do: 'I sometimes had a feeling that I was in touch with real life as I never had been before.' However, others became obsessed with the routine of caring, either to the point where they no longer felt able to participate normally in the affairs of the outside world, or where they could not cope with the mother's institutionalization or death. The majority of those immersing themselves in care were also single women who had lived with their mothers for most of their adult lives. Furthermore, their relationships with their mothers tended to be problematic, the mothers tending to be the dominating force within the household. Those who immersed themselves in caring but treated it as a challenge tended to be more in control of the situation and few of these women sought any external help. About half of those who literally lost themselves in caring received some help from kin and friends, but none received any professional help. In some cases this was due to the mistaken belief on the part of professionals that they were 'coping well'; and in some cases to the carer's inability to share her caring role. In the most extreme cases, the lack of professional support proved disastrous and the carer suffered physical and/or mental collapse.

Thus it may be seen how these three broad sets of responses relate to the particular circumstances, material and attitudinal, of each carer. What discussion of Table 7.1 cannot reveal, and what the case studies that follow do, is the way in which the relationships between the various factors that together comprise the caring process change over time. For example, the table cannot show the point at which help was offered or was withdrawn, or how the balance between kin and professional help shifted over time. To explore these kinds of issues we must return to the reconstruction of individual life experiences.

BALANCING CARE – MRS B

Mrs B, aged 58, lived with her husband and adult son. Her mother died in 1984, aged 91, a year after having been admitted to a nursing home. When her mother was widowed in the early 1960s, Mrs B, an only child, and her husband invited her mother to live with them and their two young children. The mother's dependence on Mrs B gradually increased, and by the late 1970s Mrs B had to find someone to come and stay while she and the family went on holiday, her mother neither wanting to go away nor to be left alone. In common with many of our respondents in similar positions, Mrs B found it difficult to pinpoint the beginning of this 'semi-care' period.

The transition to full-time care, however, was sudden. Mrs B's mother had a series of mini-strokes in the autumn of 1981, which caused her to become incontinent and severely restricted her mobility. This, combined with increasing confusion and deafness, meant that almost overnight Mrs B became responsible for providing full care for her mother, while struggling to continue to look after home and family, and to maintain her own outside interests. Above all, Mrs B experienced great difficulty in her attempt to maintain a 'normal' home life for her husband and son in the face of the increasing burden of caring. She viewed caring for her mother as her responsibility alone and something that should not be allowed to intrude into the lives of her own family. Her difficulties were exacerbated by the problems she experienced in finding the time or the means to seek the information and help she required. In the end her balancing act became impossible and she was faced with the guilt-laden task of finding a suitable nursing home for her mother.

Mrs B had willingly taken on the caring task which had effectively begun with her father's death: 'Once my father died we sort of took over and that was it.' There was no question about this decision: 'It was my mother. I'd do it. I always said I would never let her go into a home.' This decision did not reflect any sort of feeling of reciprocity towards Mrs B's mother. As Mrs B put it, caring was 'not in her line at all'.

From the beginning, Mrs B attempted to add the task of full-time caring to her existing responsibilities, making very little adjustment to her household routine. She set herself the task of minimizing the effects of her mother's illness on her husband and son, with the result that housework and the tasks of personal care 'took all the time'. Later in the interview, she said: 'I probably overdid trying to keep things as normal as possible. I was determined that it wasn't going to affect their lives.' This was a very similar comment to that made by another married woman carer:

> I think instead of trying to carry on a normal life with looking after mother on the side, if I'd admitted to myself that this was something I was actually doing and I'd got to make adjustments and face it head on more and go all out for the support we needed to enable us all to lead a normal life [it would have been better].

Both these respondents, who had much in common, attempted to maintain 'normality' in the face of adversity and both inferred that they were swamped by the enormity of their additional tasks. However, in frustration, both sought help and advice from GPs, nurses and others, but neither was given the help and support required to enable them to continue the caring tasks they had willingly assumed, and both incurred severe costs to their own and their families' welfare.

As for so many others, Mrs B's first point of contact was her GP. The male doctors in the group practice took the view that her problems would eventually right themselves and that there was little to be done. Mrs B usually waited to attend the surgery until she knew she could see the woman doctor, whom she found more supportive, although not particularly informative. Mrs B was faced with the task of finding out information about social security and the attendance allowance; how to deal with aspects of physical tending such as bathing, lifting, and the use of a catheter; and about respite care facilities, at precisely the same time that she was swamped by the minutiae of the caring routines required to deal with an incapacitated, confused elderly person, in addition to the needs of her husband and son. Mrs B had great difficulty in obtaining information: 'If you've never

come up against it you just don't know what's available and if
nobody tells you you don't know. I understand some GPs do a
lot more. . . . I didn't even know I'd got a health visitor, which
sounds naive. . . . ' Obtaining access to information is a crucial
first hurdle for people who have never cared for an old person
before, and seems to depend on the carer having the luck to come
across a service provider who will refer her to other sources of
help. As it was, Mrs B claimed not to have had either the time or
the means to seek out advice: 'The people in authority think
they've got a lot to offer you, but they don't worry about how
you're going to get to them.'

The problem for Mrs B was not only finding out about and
obtaining assistance, but the fact that when it became available,
help was often offered on terms that made it difficult or inconvenient for her to accept it. The first help she received, as a result
of her mother's strokes, came from district nurses who came to
help her bath her mother. But this arrangement was eventually
discontinued for two main reasons. First, when younger nurses
replaced the older, more experienced ones, Mrs B felt that she
knew as much or more about handling old people as they did.
Second, she never knew when they were coming and for her and
her mother established routines were a vital way of managing the
caring task. Mrs B's experience of using a day centre was similar
in that, while she was in this case very appreciative of the work of
the centre (recommended to her by the health visitor), she ended
up having to chauffeur her mother to and fro because they were
not on the ambulance route, thus eating into the time made available for her other tasks.

Mrs B found the night nursing required for a confused, incontinent person particularly difficult, but received little help: 'Night
times were terrible. She'd wake up in the night, full of beans –
turn out everything, pull out the catheter. I got into trouble
because I called out the night nurse for the catheter.' Eventually
Mrs B wrote to the health authority about the problem, and the
authority confirmed her right to call on the nurse: 'At last I was
beginning to stand up for myself.' Not surprisingly, Mrs B perceived her attempt to secure help from professionals in terms of a
constant struggle.

Mrs B desperately needed, but did not receive, support and
reinforcement in her attempt to balance caring for her mother with
that for her family, as well as for her efforts to sustain outside

interests, including a part-time degree course. In particular she needed help in understanding her mother's mental and physical deterioration, especially in respect to her then adolescent son, who watched the grandmother he had known all his life change into a different and alien person. Until her mother's series of strokes in 1981, Mrs B felt that she had 'bridged the gap' between the generations fairly successfully. But her son withdrew as his grandmother deteriorated and to Mrs B's knowledge has never talked about how he felt. Nor did he ever visit his grandmother once she was in the nursing home. The role of Mrs B's husband is not clear. He worked long hours and Mrs B clearly felt it her duty to keep the burden of caring hidden from him. However, it was he who finally persuaded Mrs B that the situation had to change. Mrs B had had only one two-week break in the year when her mother went into hospital for respite care, and her mental health was beginning to suffer under the strain. In view of her effort to continue activities such as her university course, this carer would have benefited enormously from a weekly break.

Mrs B had no kin or other immediate family who could have helped. However, she was fortunate in having several old friends, one of whom had cared for her own mother and who provided moral support throughout the caring period. Mrs B's positive attitudes towards these friends stood in marked contrast to her perceptions of her neighbours: 'It was [the] people from my past who were much more helpful. Everyone around here goes out to work.' She seemed ambivalent when asked about the kind of help neighbours might have provided: 'For ordinary day support, it's surprising how many people when they find out what the problem is, it's an elderly person, a bit unpredictable, let's put it, are not quite so willing to come. [Were you hesitant to ask for help?] Yes, I was, because I never knew what would happen.' Her comments reveal the limitations of assumptions that are often made about the existence or potential of neighbourhood 'networks'. Regardless of whether it is the carer or the neighbour who is reluctant to seek involvement, it is clear from this and many other examples that mental deterioration and incontinence proved almost insurmountable barriers either to requesting or accepting help from neighbours or others only casually acquainted with the persons caring and cared for.

Mrs B herself seems to have coped with the deterioration in her mother's mental state and in the quality of their relationship by

distancing herself from her mother. A relationship that had probably always been subject to tensions, but that was nevertheless
deeply felt, became increasingly problematic after 1981. Mrs B
admitted to the interviewer over coffee – while the tape-recorder
was switched off – that she managed to continue caring for her
mother only by treating her as a 'different person'. However, the
most difficult part for Mrs B was taking the step which she had
vowed she never would and admitting her mother to a home: 'I
always said I'd never let her go into a home. But I couldn't have
kept going without it affecting my husband and son a bit more.'

Finding a suitable home was very difficult. The only help she
received was to be given a list of homes, but on closer examination she found that many of them would not cater for an elderly
person with senile dementia, incontinence, and considerable
physical incapacity. The relief Mrs B felt at the ending of the task
of physically caring for her mother was tempered by the guilt and
worry she felt about the home she finally chose: 'I found this
place which, looking back on it, was not ideal. But after a lot of
heart-searching, that's what we decided . . . it's not a step I
would take . . . [fade away].' She was able to share this to some
extent with other people who visited the home, but the tie to and
feeling of responsibility for her mother only really ended when
her mother died.

Despite the difficulties she had faced in caring, by the time of
the interview Mrs B was in fact already 'picking up the pieces' in
a constructive way. She had given up her degree course when
her mother entered the nursing home, probably because of
accumulated stress. Mrs B's husband had certainly felt that she
had reached breaking point, and was instrumental in making the
decision to admit her mother to a home. It is not clear that left to
herself Mrs B would have either recognized or admitted the need
to take this step. After her mother's death she recommenced her
course and returned to her former clubs and social activities, and
is concentrating on getting her home back to normal. The stresses
caused by her effort to maintain these activities during the period
of caring have been justified after caring ended by the way in
which they have enabled her effectively to restructure her life.

Thus the very difficult effort to balance caring with previous
commitments and activities may have long-term value for the
carer, who in the end may have the satisfaction of having cared
for as long as possible, but who has also maintained other sources

of self-worth or identity to turn to when the caring ends. This may be compared to the experience of those who 'immersed' themselves in caring, often to the exclusion of all else, with consequent long-term difficulties in adjusting to the end of co-resident care. But in order to perform such a balancing act it is clear that the carer and person cared for require more than simple medical assistance, help with tasks such as bathing, or day care support. Practical help must be offered in a way that respects the integrity and dignity of both the carer and elderly person. Mrs B felt strongly that she was 'taken as being hands free and . . . able' with little or no acknowledgement given to her efforts to sustain other activities of great importance to her. Help for the carer should recognize and support – practically and emotionally – the carer's desires to maintain an existence and identity of her own.

INTEGRATING CARE – MISS C

Miss C, aged 68, always lived with her mother, except during the war. A period of semi-care began in 1966 when Miss C's mother had a stroke and lost some use of one leg and a hand. She needed help with cooking and bathing. But the two went on holiday together and Miss C continued in her job as a civil servant, working flexi-hours and occasionally bringing work home.

In 1978, the situation changed. Miss C retired naturally at age 60 in that year, although she said that her mother's worsening condition would have necessitated this in any case; she referred to 'exchanging one job for another'. In 1979, her mother had a bad heart attack, and was bedridden, immobile upstairs, for fifteen months. She died in 1981, aged 98.

Miss C's caring tasks were similar to those of many of our respondents, involving full physical care, but she approached them in a fairly relaxed and philosophical way: 'I consciously decided that it was no good moaning or groaning because I couldn't do this or that, so I decided to be an opportunist.' Her ability to do this may well have resulted from the relationship which she and her mother had created and enjoyed over the years. Miss C's mother was quite dominant within the home, but this suited Miss C, who was out at work all day. Miss C had clearly achieved a working relationship with her mother, in which each party appreciated the other's strengths and sensitivities. Both sometimes felt impatient at the constraints imposed by their situation:

'I used to say, "You are an old nagger", and she used to say, "I'm not", but it was all in good part.' Ultimately Miss C was able to say: 'Our relationship wasn't ruined by the caring.'

In addition to this relationship, Miss C reported constructive sources of support which played a major part in ensuring that caring was not perceived by her as a unique burden. She remembered the GP as 'marvellous' (he had reassured her that she had done the best possible for her mother), and the district nurses as having provided valuable support, albeit variable in terms of its quality and quantity. She was able to call on the support of a married sister, although she clearly felt that this sister had not provided enough practical support, and described the way in which a friend had mediated on her behalf, after which the sister stayed overnight once a week. When her mother went to stay with the sister for periods of respite care, neither the mother nor Miss C were very happy with the care the sister provided. Despite the expression of her feeling that she had been let down by her sister, there was an element of mutual reward between her mother and herself which might have operated to the exclusion of the sister.

It appears above all that Miss C's friends offered practical and moral support to both Miss C and her mother. Miss C paid a 'local friend' to help settle her mother into bed every night, and a sense of communality and pride permeated her account of how together they managed to stop her mother from developing bedsores. Friends also 'brought my social life in', which delighted her mother as well. Miss C's mother, who suffered physical, not mental, disability, remained alert and interested in her own appearance and in her daughter's life throughout the caring period, and she welcomed visits from people she knew, although she resisted help from strangers or sitters. Miss C might have welcomed these, but was in part resigned to doing without and in part happy to indulge her mother in this as in all aspects of their domestic life: while a 'lady of great spirit', her mother was nevertheless vulnerable as someone in need of her care and attention. It seems that an open, welcoming atmosphere was the chief characteristic of this household. Miss C's caring tasks were demanding, but this open atmosphere and the frequent presence of friends meant that caring did not become a burden isolated from normal life. On the contrary, Miss C's everyday contacts seem to have been brought into the household.

Despite her illness, Miss C's mother co-operated in her care:

'She was a bit sensitive about me having to do everything, but then I think she realized there was nothing for it . . . she was so reasonable.' All this was not without cost to Miss C, but it appears to be a cost which had its rewards: 'I was tied obviously, I couldn't live the life I might otherwise have lived.' Miss C referred specifically to missed opportunities for promotion. But from the first she seems to have felt that the obverse of caring was companionship, which she greatly valued and also felt gratified in performing a task for which only she was needed: 'I like to be needed, it sounds silly but . . . ' Miss C felt above all that her work as a carer had been appreciated by her mother, her friends, and her GP. When her mother died Miss C experienced some difficulty in coming to terms with her loss: 'When you've lost someone who had been very close, because in the case of mother and daughter circumstances . . . you do become the pivot of their lives. . . . When you're not that any more your own evaluation [of yourself] is diminished.'

But with friends to hand, Miss C has been able to build on her caring experiences and now works with a carer's group and in advice work. She gained great personal satisfaction from looking after her mother until she died, helped especially by her mother's co-operative attitude and by her good friends who offered constant support. There were inevitably pains and hardships, but these were mitigated by the supportiveness of the mother/daughter relationship and close support from friends, whom she feels she will be able to count on for some considerable time to come.

IMMERSION IN CARING – MISS A

Miss A, aged 58, had lived all her life with her mother, with whom she had been 'great friends'. When her father died in 1958, she moved with her mother from their family home in central London to a house in the suburbs; her brother, his wife and son also moved nearby. Thus although old family ties had been left behind, a small extended family supported each other, and Miss A's mother looked after her grandson while Miss A and her brother and sister-in-law went out to work.

A series of events occurred which led eventually to Miss A assuming total responsibility for her mother, who was becoming increasingly incapacitated through senile dementia. Miss A's brother moved away with his firm, at about the same time as his son married and also moved away. The immediate family thus broke up at exactly the same time as Miss A's mother became more incapacitated. In 1980, two years before her mother died, Miss A took early retirement, which she might have had to do anyway because of redundancies at her firm. With few local friends or contacts (she had worked in central London), and with her immediate family moved away, Miss A then immersed herself (not unwillingly) in the task of caring for her mother. For the last eighteen months of her life, Miss A's mother required constant care, but her previously companionate relationship with her daughter changed, as the senile dementia worsened. At her brother's insistence, Miss A finally admitted her mother to a private nursing home in 1982, and one month later her mother died in hospital. About a month after that, Miss A had a complete breakdown, from which she was only just recovering at the time of the interview.

With hindsight, Miss A could herself see that she had cut herself off from outside contacts, had retired from work, and seen her immediate family disperse, all contributing to her eventual breakdown. When asked what advice she would give to others, she responded: 'I'd impress on them not to give up all their friends even if it was only on the 'phone. You mustn't immerse yourself in just the two of you. You don't think of it at the time.' She had not been an unwilling carer, but she did feel there were ways in which she could have been helped, particularly by her brother: 'I felt he should have 'phoned me more often than he did. He probably thought, "Oh, she's capable, she can get on with it." I mean he had a very demanding job. I felt he could have shown more concern.'

Miss A was an admitted introvert who had given little consideration to her future when she drifted into caring for her mother. She commented with hindsight: 'I think I should have perhaps made more of a life for myself.' But the inexorable increase in the burden of caring, together with her already narrow horizons, meant that her own needs were subjugated to those of the caring task, and to those of her mother, who had had few friends and who, after her husband died, relied on her daughter for everything.

The semi-care period had started with her mother's widowhood: 'I suppose I used to feel guilty about going out after my father died. I used to go on holiday with her because I thought she wouldn't have a holiday if I didn't go with her.' This semi-care period was a companionate phase in which both mother and daughter were content, supported by and supporting a small extended family. At about the time the family moved away, symptoms of senility were developing, and the balance of the relationship began to change until, towards the end, the mother did not recognize Miss A at all: 'In a way, I was her whole life really. And that was why it was so sad when she really didn't know me, you know?'

The semi-care period lasted until Miss A left work. As in several of our 'caring biographies', it is difficult here to be sure of cause and effect. We feel fairly sure that in several cases caring has been rationalized as a cause for changes in respondents' lives which might in fact have occurred for other reasons, in this case because the respondent's firm was asking for early retirement and Miss A thought she might have been asked to go. However, regardless of its true cause, retirement had two immediate effects: Miss A's mother became less able to care for herself, deferring to her daughter, and Miss A missed her previous contacts at work, particularly male companionship, which she enjoyed and found stimulating. Miss A was well compensated on retirement, had a good pension and her mother received the attendance allowance; income was not a problem.

Miss A increasingly immersed herself in caring. She saw a man friend infrequently because, 'You see, to see him, I had to get somebody in to see my mother', and although for a while the local authority provided an occasional (irregular) granny-sitting service, Miss A said she still 'had an eye on the clock' and felt that she did not want to 'take advantage', 'overstaying your welcome, you know, that sort of thing'.

Miss A's mother required little medical care and although a nurse visited occasionally and ensured that supplies such as incontinence pads were plentiful, there was little opportunity for contact with anyone who might have been able to help Miss A recognize and deal with the imbalance developing in her own life. Even the provision of respite care, so desperately sought by many of our respondents, did not by itself enable Miss A to pursue an independent interest after a lifetime of sharing with her mother. After a week's holiday, she returned home, visited her mother in hospital, was consumed with guilt at finding her crying, and took her home. Miss A was unable to take advantage of her unaccustomed freedom and in her case, as in that of Mrs B, it might have been more satisfactory to arrange regular weekly breaks to give her a chance to develop a sustained outside interest which would have stood her in good stead when the caring ended.

Miss A's case is a good example of how a person with few existing outside interests, and with limited expectations, can become totally involved in the caring task: 'I think I just accepted how she was. I didn't have the time to think about it really. You know, one doesn't. One doesn't have the time. Your mind is completely on them.' During the period of full care, kin were distant and not as supportive as she would have liked; practical help was available but not backed by any kind of emotional or counselling support; her personal life was narrowed by retirement; and what contacts she might have had were constrained by her reluctance to use sitting services regularly for fear of 'taking advantage'. Her day was filled with looking after her mother. When asked about free time she said: 'It was just a case of nine o'clock in the morning, dashing up to the shop and dashing back again with my eye on the watch all the time.' Although Miss A paid agency nurses occasionally so that she could go out, there is little evidence that she used this time to develop her own separate interests.

As the caring period progressed, Miss A derived a sense of satisfaction and worth from her role as carer, although this was somewhat diminished by the gradual erosion of her previously close relationship with her mother. Towards the end she reported that it was impossible to 'get through' to her mother, which made her irritable and, in turn, guilty. She found herself blurting out things in anger and frustration that she later regretted, for example: 'I'm not going to give up all my friends like you did.' In all probability Miss A saw her mother as isolated, but despite recognizing the problem ended up in the same situation herself.

As her mother's condition deteriorated, and the physical strain of caring for her increased, Miss A came under pressure from her brother to have her mother admitted to a home. Fearing a withdrawal of his slender support, Miss A reluctantly acquiesced. This was clearly difficult for her, for she (perhaps not consciously at this point) found it very threatening to relinquish her role as carer. Miss A reported that her mother had always said she did

not want to be a burden on anyone and that she was quite prepared to go to hospital, but so much of Miss A's identity was
invested in the caring role that even after her mother went into a
home, she said she 'couldn't switch off'. Although she was
firmly discouraged from visiting by the nursing home, Miss A
visited more or less daily until, a month later, her mother died.

> When she was alive, I was fully taken up with looking after
> her. When she died there was nothing, just nothing. I just
> went to pieces then. I thought whatever am I going to do with
> the rest of my life – I just completely folded up. It was basically
> loneliness really.

After a complete breakdown and residential treatment, Miss A
has gradually, deliberately, begun to construct a new life for herself
revolving around voluntary work with a variety of local agencies.
She felt that one contributory factor to her breakdown was her
desire to keep a stiff upper lip: 'I always like to keep a brave face. I
didn't like people to know I was down. I think I kept so much to
myself this is what brought on the breakdown.' She finds it impossible to think about her own future because she finds the thought of
being alone in her old age too depressing to deal with.

For supporters of the carers there is clearly a difficult task here
to decide when the 'brave face' is a facade masking a tightly controlled situation which could well lead to eventual breakdown.
Where the social activities of the carer have been dropped completely, it may be that the most appropriate form of help will be
that which provides both the opportunity *and* the moral support
for the carer to have some time to call her own, and not to feel
guilty at using this time for her personal development. In a few
cases we found that voluntary mutual support groups gave great
help to carers. But often these groups do not have the resources
to provide substitute care so that their members can attend
meetings. Financial support to enable this might prove a valuable
saving in the long run, if these provisions enabled carers to share
their experiences and meet other people with a common interest.

THE CARING MATRIX AND THE CARING
SEQUENCE

Every 'caring biography' will be unique. In presenting these
three, we do not propose that they are in any way 'typical' – only

that they allow us to develop certain themes about factors which contribute to the development of the caring sequence and how carers may respond to these factors. It is our view that it is difficult to prescribe appropriate help or support without an appreciation of the carer's position: how she is personally dealing with the stresses confronting her, and how these interact with the views of the person cared for.

The 'Caring Matrix' (Fig. 7.1) is therefore designed to show the various elements that determine the caring experience. These vary for each carer and person cared for. Each matrix is a mix of relationships, circumstances and attitudes, and begins at a unique point for each caring pair, although changes in the matrix after this point may proceed in similar ways.

Figure 7.1 Co-resident caring matrix

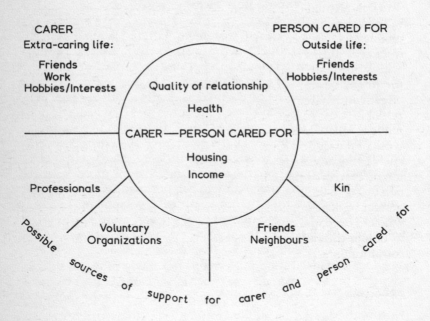

During the caring period, the changes in the balance of the caring matrix may bring, or be prompted by, changes in the nature of the caring task. Thus, for instance, if incontinence develops, the person cared for may feel degraded or embarrassed; may not wish to see former friends; may not accept strangers to help with the problem; may deny the problem or not co-operate in helping to treat it, either through wilfulness or through the effects of illness. For the carer, parallel changes may occur. Almost certainly, the caring task becomes more demanding, with increased washing and cleaning up; the carer may not know of, or wish to seek, professional help; the carer may feel revulsion, and not feel able to invite friends in, or to ask neighbours to 'lend a hand'. For each person this new situation may produce a sequence of events which increases workload, tension, and anxiety. This in turn may alter the relationship between carer and person cared for, and may also alter the balance of relationships in the caring matrix.

The caring matrix is particularly useful for the way in which it enables us to conceptualize the kinds of changes in caring relationships during the caring period. It thus provides supporters with some insight into how problems of carers and people cared for might be approached when they are considering ways of effectively enabling the caring task to be continued with least possible stress to carer and person cared for. Thus efforts may be made to relieve balancers of some of the conflict they feel between work or family and caring, and immersers may be offered help in such a way as not to threaten their role as carer, while encouraging them to maintain some outside interest. Carers who *appear* to be coping, whether integrators or immersers, may be in more danger of neglect and subsequent health breakdown than those who are prepared to articulate their difficulties, often in an effort to obtain the help necessary to balance caring with their other commitments.

Semi-care

During the period of semi-care, the designation of the carer is already clear. The lives of the carer and person cared for may retain considerable independence of each other, although in some cases we found mothers who were wholly dependent on their daughters even at this stage for social, emotional, and practical support. The caring task entails more by way of a sense of responsibility than demanding caring tasks, and each person may retain friendships and activities outside their immediate relationship. The carer may be working, but is unlikely to be exhausted, under constant strain, or embarrassed by her mother's condition. Social life is restricted by the semi-care tie, but friends may still visit or be visited, and while career progress may be constrained by the tie, there is otherwise little restriction. If the carer is married and has a family, it is likely that the other members of the family will either share the responsibility for the dependent person or form a relationship with her.

For the person cared for, there is still a sense of independence, of being able to carry on with normal household tasks. There is possibly pain or discomfort relating to physical health, but usually not severe incapacity. She is probably widowed, but may retain contact with friends.

At this stage, the relationship between the carer and person cared for will largely be based on its past history, although the way in which the decision was made to commence the period of semi-care may affect both participants' perceptions of the relationship. It is possible that outside agencies are already involved, for instance in the provision of occasional nursing care.

The semi-care tie may also characterize the period following the carer's decision to opt for some form of institutional care for the person cared for. At this time, the carer's feelings of love and duty are overlaid with feelings of guilt at having admitted the dependant to a home or hospital. Relationships with staff at the institution may be crucial in enabling both carer and person cared for to adjust to this new phase. In most cases, our respondents found it difficult to let go of the caring tie, and continued not only to visit but also to worry about their mothers' care.

Part-time full care

For carers at work, the step into part-time full care may be gradual and almost unnoticed, or triggered by an event such as a stroke or progress of senile dementia to a stage where the dependant is no longer able to be responsible for herself. For carers not engaged in paid employment and with family commitments, the lines between semi-care, part-time full care, and full care are more difficult to draw. However, during the period of part-time full care both sets of carers assume a heavier burden, which involves much more complicated planning to accommodate both the carer's needs and those of the dependant. Involvement at work may provide an external source of stimulation and satisfaction, but brings its own strains: fear of losing the job, particularly if the employer or colleagues are not sympathetic; fear of the financial consequences of giving up work, and of loss of status; and sometimes the strain of maintaining a facade of normality at work.

Neighbours and friends who had previously dropped in as part of a normal social routine may withdraw as the caring tasks become more demanding or perhaps distasteful. The carer may become isolated, with little time for anything but work and care.

The carer may find out about services from GPs or nurses, or from a social worker. Others may not know where to turn and may not be supported by well-informed professionals. Pressures of time on the carer and the inability to leave the person cared for can preclude opportunities for finding out about available help. In some cases the carer and/or person cared for may not be amenable to offers of help from external agencies. In others, the carer may be a 'coper' and determined to rise to the challenge, nevertheless experiencing some increased stress and pressure as the demands of work and caring take their toll.

The person cared for may also experience changes in attitude and perception including more sense of being a burden; increased pain and fear; and anxiety about the nature of the illness or disability. These may also be accompanied by a sense of humiliation or degradation, and a fear or dislike of strangers performing personal tasks or intruding in a home where strangers may never have been particularly welcome.

As the primary caring relationship grows in intensity, both the carer and person cared for may experience additional strain if their accommodation is cramped or otherwise unsuitable for caring. Both may lack privacy.

Full care

Full care is similar to part-time full care except that the carer is devoted entirely to the task of caring. The balance of a married woman's efforts now tips firmly in favour of the elderly person. In many cases care for other family members is reduced to the essentials of material maintenance, with the result that emotional relationships with husband and children suffer. For (the primarily single) carers who have struggled to keep their jobs, full care may remove an element of stress, as the carer no longer has to balance demands of work and home. At the same time it can contribute to financial hardship and isolation for both carer and person cared for.

The involvement of friends and neighbours remains problematic: how to ask for help, and what work can reasonably be expected of helpers, are both ill defined. The role of outside agencies becomes crucial during this period. They must now help with caring tasks, and may also provide the only link between the carer and the outside world. This situation requires sensitive assessment on the part of supporters and both the carer and person cared for need practical and emotional support they can rely on.

The carer's physical and mental health may begin to deteriorate just as the condition of the person cared for worsens, and the end of this stage in the caring period is reached either with the death of the dependant, or a decision to admit her to an institution. Both of these events require that sympathetic support be given to the carer.

For the person cared for, there may be increasing fear, especially if the condition is terminal. It is possible that neither the carer nor person cared for are able to articulate their feelings about this. The dependant may also feel increasing pain, humiliation, and a sense of burden and guilt. During this period it is no longer possible for the person cared for to make her accustomed contribution to the household, and how well she adapts to this may play a significant part in determining whether the primary caring relationship continues to be mutually supportive or whether problems either develop or significantly increase. The nature of the illness may preclude successful adaptation and add to the strain for both parties.

Recovery from caring

For the carer, the death of the person cared for will introduce a grieving period which also often includes difficult adjustment to a new role. If all outside life has been excluded during the period of full care, this adjustment may be particularly difficult. The carer may feel a loss of purpose, or a sense of time lost and opportunities missed.

If the person cared for is admitted to an institution, the carer may also experience a loss of purpose. In addition she may resent handing over the valued role of carer to others who appear not to care so much; and will probably feel guilt at having handed over care at all.

For the person cared for, admission to an institution can occasionally result in some improvement, for instance in cases where the person cared for had manipulated the carer to gain attention and services she was still capable of performing herself, or where she had suffered grave anxiety as to the burden of care she was imposing on her daughter. In every case, the relationship between carer, person cared for, and new carers in the institution becomes a complex mix.

CHAPTER 8

The legacy of caring

All the women in our sample had responded to the injunction to care. One described the way that she, together with a group of ex-carers, had decided that they were 'the type of person' that cared:

> You're either the sort that can turn your back on it and say well, I'm going off to lead my life, or the type that gets caught up in it and however much you protest, and it really does take more out of you than you want to give, if you're that type of person you go on doing it . . . you find it quite impossible to walk away from doing it.

However, experiences of caring varied widely. This same respondent also said: 'From then on until she died, fifteen months, it was just get up in the morning, take some aspirins, grit your teeth and get on somehow.' In contrast another recalled: 'We did have a rapport that was quite extraordinary . . . we didn't have to say very much, just sit happily in the same room.'

The legacy of caring reflects *both* the commitment to caring felt by most carers and the kinds of difficulties the carer may experience at the everyday level in dealing with the tasks of caring and the changing quality of the caring relationship, and in fitting caring into their lives. Thus the legacy of caring is profoundly ambivalent. While almost all carers said they were glad that they had cared, they also often experienced loneliness and loss of purpose; difficulty in 'picking up the pieces'; residual bitterness about the behaviour of kin, lack of services, financial help, and lost opportunities; and anxiety about their own old age.

Respondents were in very different stages of adjustment to the end of co-resident caring at the time of the interviews. In six cases the mother was still alive and in a home or hospital and in eleven cases the mother had died within the previous two years. The feelings of those respondents might be expected to be very different from those whose mothers had died some five to ten years earlier. Nevertheless the degree to which respondents experience lasting bitterness, or loss of purpose in particular, appears to vary enormously and, we would suggest, may to some extent be predicted from the nature of the caring experience and the way in which its end is managed. Broadly, those who immersed themselves in caring were likely to experience extreme difficulty in adjusting to the end of co-resident care; those who struggled to balance caring with other responsibilities were likely to feel a sense of both relief and guilt; and those who managed to integrate caring into their lives tended to experience the most profound sense of loss.

Some respondents, but by no means all, had reworked their experiences for themselves and had achieved a greater understanding of them in the period between their mother's death and the interview. In some cases this enabled respondents to achieve a greater peace, in others it served to increase resentment. One respondent, for example, only recognized the extent to which she had been dominated by her mother after the latter died: 'I did care for her, I did care about her and I felt terribly sorry for her ... but I didn't need her.... I didn't realize that until she was dead.' Her mother's death brought a great sense of liberation, but also a deepening resentment about the 'lost years'. There were also instances of respondents attributing all their personal regrets and failures to the fact that they had been tied to caring for their mothers even though in four cases the respondents' own narratives revealed that this was clearly a distorted perception. It was nevertheless a real source of bitterness for those concerned.

ADJUSTING TO THE END OF CO-RESIDENT CARE

The most common problem at the end of the period of full-time co-resident care was the gap it left in respondents' lives. Respondents usually experienced a loss of purpose that proved very disorienting. This feeling faded with time as new routines were established, although loneliness often persisted. In the case of a respondent whose mother had entered an institution a year before the interview, the daughter was still experiencing difficulty in coming to terms with the loss of her identity as carer: 'In a way I miss the responsibility you know. It was something that I did. I was somebody who looked after their mother, I had a sort of purpose.' This type of feeling was particularly strong in those who had immersed themselves in the care of their mothers. A respondent whose mother had died three years previously commented: 'I seem to fill my time with nothing, I don't know', while Miss A, as we have seen, suffered a bad breakdown on her mother's death: 'When she died there was nothing, just nothing.' The dangers of immersion in caring when it is accompanied by increasing isolation from all outside activities and when the carer is not well supported by either kin or professionals are great. Even for those who did gradually come to appreciate their new freedom, the adjustment was painful.

> You don't have to be somebody's daughter, you can be you. And it does, it takes a lot of getting used to – and how you'd be if you weren't working – if I'd have done what I was told and packed up my job I don't know what I'd have done, because at least having to go to work you went to work and had so much to do you didn't think and it helped you over the bad patches.

Loss of purpose took a less destructive form in those for whom their mothers had been companions and for whom caring had filled a gap in their lives. We have described these carers, the vast majority of them single women, as having practised a similar kind of division of labour to that of husbands and wives as long as the condition of their mothers permitted. When their mothers died these women experienced a profound sense of loss. One said that when she comes back from holiday: 'I don't have to phone anyone, you don't belong to anyone any more.' Miss C, whose story was considered in the last chapter, said something very similar:

> One of the things I suppose I felt . . . one of the difficult things to come to terms with, is the fact you're going out and no one really cares whether you come back or not, well, that's an exaggeration, but you don't come first with anyone.

A respondent whose mother had entered a home and who visited her frequently spoke vehemently about feeling bereft:

When I visit she always comes to the door and I kiss her good-night and she waves and says when are you coming again and it's an awful feeling, especially in the winter, and I think she is nice and snug and cosy and warm and I'm going home to – I go there on the way from work, I leave at 7.30, and going home, it's a horrible feeling then, horrible going to an empty house.

These women had managed either to keep working or had kept up friendships, and their identities were not so heavily invested in caring that they experienced a loss of purpose amounting to an identity crisis. However, they experienced considerable difficulty in adjusting to both the lack of companionship and the fact that they were no longer needed by someone else: 'And it is difficult because whereas before that there was somebody else to consider and somebody else to think about, and there's nobody there, just you.'

Feelings of loneliness often persisted and again tended to be particularly severe for those who had immersed themselves in caring. One woman who experienced a prolonged period of caring let friendships slide.

What have you got to write about except illness and nobody wants to hear that all the time. You see if you go out and do something you've got something to write about or if you've got children to write about . . . so I gradually let them fall. I do find it now.

Others spoke of their fear of being on their own and the difficulty in deciding to do anything when they had no ties, 'no pull anywhere'.

The intensity of the caring experience, especially during the (usually) final period of full-time care, sometimes meant that the carer, whether or not immersed in caring or experiencing a supportive relationship with her mother or not, found it extremely difficult to deal with life beyond the private world of caring after it was all over. One of a pair of sisters who cared for their mother gave up her job to devote herself to caring and after the mother died found it very difficult to apply for the kind of jobs she had done before, eventually settling for a low-grade clerical job. Two married women who had struggled to balance caring with their family responsibilities also experienced a severe loss of confidence in respect to doing things outside the home after the caring period ended. One felt that she had lost the kind of contacts that had provided her with spiritual and cultural inspiration. After her mother died she found it crucial to find a group of people with whom she could 'go out and talk about caring' and the way in which it had both enriched her life and narrowed her horizons. The other reported crossing the street rather than meet someone after her mother's death: 'I began to feel very insecure . . . to lose complete confidence in myself.' About eighteen months later she happened to see an advertisement in the paper for a welfare assistant and successfully applied for the job. 'It's possibly the best thing I did. . . . This tremendous feeling of uselessness was with me a long time . . . if I'd left it any longer I wouldn't actually have had the motivation to do it.' Almost all carers were left to deal with these crises of confidence, identity and purpose, and loneliness by themselves. The GP of one gave her some sleeping pills, while that of another counselled her briskly: ' "Get a good night's sleep and get back to normal life again, that's all you need. " . . . I felt like kicking him in the teeth.' Lack of any counselling usually served to perpetuate both the carer's anxiety about the way she felt and the depression concomitant with bereavement.

Remarkably few carers expressed unalloyed relief at the end of co-resident care, even though professionals often appeared to assume that this would be their predominant feeling, especially in cases where the mother was being taken into institutional care and the burden of care removed from the carer. The married women who were concerned about their families and the single women about their work tended to express some relief that it was all over. In general, these women did not wish to care in the same way for anyone else. Some expressed relief at not having to worry about what they might come home and find. 'I suppose I felt a certain amount of relief, but also guilt', was a common statement, or 'relief yes, but sadness too'. Those who had experienced problematic relationships with their mothers sometimes felt that they were at last free to be themselves, but also felt extremely disoriented, especially when the mother had been the dominant party.

Thus 'picking up the pieces' – a phrase often used by respondents – was by no means easy after full-time caring stopped:

I was in such a mess. I couldn't concentrate. I made myself learn to read all over again, believe it or not. And I got a library book. I thought that's got to go back in a month, so let's have a start and that first page was read and re-read and re-read and it was real uphill work, trying even to take it in it was. [Has that improved?] Oh yes, I'm still slow at getting through the books, but it does go in now, yes, I've conquered that . . . and I do go along to classes.

This respondent had obviously come close to a breakdown in the final stages of her mother's care, and four years later was still experiencing considerable difficulty in performing everyday tasks. In less extreme cases, carers tried to rebuild friendships, resume their jobs or activities they had enjoyed, but not always with success even after considerable time had elapsed. Two spoke of the need to come to terms with the fact that some activities could not be resumed because too much time had passed, or because the carer's own health was not what it had once been: 'You find that things had changed. . . . And you lose skills.' This respondent had tried going back to her art class, but found that her own eyesight had deteriorated too much for her to continue. In such instances the feeling that it was therefore impossible to make up for the time lost can turn into bitterness.

However other respondents were able to revel in some aspects of their new situation: 'I think I delighted in doing things for the sake of it, just sitting over breakfast – not hurrying, watching TV, reading the paper – and not doing anything to order.' Some acknowledged that in their battles for access to services they had grown more assertive and as a result two had become particularly active organizers of carers' associations. Four others became deeply involved in voluntary organizations, one to the extent that she reported not being able to book a holiday because of the meetings she was involved in. Carers who had retired or who had given up work to care often seem to have found that work on behalf of voluntary organizations provided a much-needed structure for their daily lives, replacing the routine of caring and to some extent carrying on the work of caring. One had decided to marry a much older person, something she herself identified as a continuation of her desire to care. Ten of our respondents 'carried on caring' for other relatives after their mothers died, although usually at a distance. In one case, the respondent reported going to visit an elderly woman friend of her mother. They had used to meet once a fortnight when her mother was alive; she now visits once a week: 'I cling to her as part of the old regime . . . I call her my second mother.' Another had helped to assuage her grief at losing her mother by supporting an old friend whose wife was dying:

> I was so glad I was able to be there [at the friend's wife's death]. . . . I was able to help him. He was utterly undomesticated. I treated him like a young brother. Then lo and behold he had a heart attack last July and he died in his sleep early in December. And that's been a bitter blow. . . . But I did manage to keep [his] dog. . . . So now I've got to get used to being on my own with an animal. . . . He's settled down wonderfully. And of course he's a great companion. I mustn't get too fond of him – My dear, let me get you a cup of tea.

The last sentence was rushed into the conversation as this 'vocation carer' realized her own vulnerability in respect to the dog. A significant number of our respondents kept pets of some kind.

Even those who had successfully picked up the pieces were not unlikely to feel residual bitterness about some aspect of the caring experience. Some felt an overwhelming sense of missed opportunities. Two were very sorry that they had not had children, although it is not clear that they would have married had they not been caring. In neither case did they attempt to leave home. Another felt that she had not been able to marry her fiancé, yet the fiancé was perfectly willing to accept her mother and she seems to have made the decision to opt for her job, her mother, and her fiancé in that order, her chance of marriage disappearing when her fiancé died before her mother. Similarly, several respondents felt that they had sacrificed possibilities of job advancement or travel abroad, but perhaps more prevalent than such specific concerns was a more general feeling of a lack of opportunity 'to catch up on any sort of life for myself'. Those who had balanced caring with family or work responsibilities felt they had been on a treadmill for years and had had little or no time for any personal growth. This in part was the root of the sudden loss of confidence sometimes experienced at the end of the caring period.

The sense of claustrophobia and a realization of the way their lives had been very narrow for many years induced great residual bitterness in some. One woman was quite adamant that she would never choose to go through it again: 'Oh no I wouldn't,

I'd get out of the house, I'd go and get any sort of job . . . anything rather than have that sort of life again. . . . Oh no, I'd never do it again.' This woman was very unusual in her complete lack of any sense of positive satisfaction from caring, although her feelings of being trapped by caring were only stronger in degree than those of several others. Three carers felt completely negative about their experiences, two because of the way in which the sense of claustrophobia was compounded by their dominant and uncooperative mothers, who made it extremely difficult for them to have any life of their own. The third again experienced a very bad relationship with her mother:

> [It was] quite wrong of me to have done it at all because she wouldn't accept that I had to help her . . . and I – I – that was a job I don't think I was able to do and I did what I would laughingly call my best and I don't think it was good enough. I didn't achieve anything for either of us, it didn't help [my husband], it was a disaster quite frankly.

While the majority did not feel that their lives had been irretrievably marred in some way by caring, many were still bitter about some aspect of it, for instance the failure on the part of kin or the state to provide adequate support. In a sense the only reward that attaches to caring is 'appreciation', by the person being cared for, kin, friends and neighbours, and professional helpers. Many carers felt wholly or partly unappreciated and believed that their tasks could have been made much easier had more support been forthcoming. Criticism of siblings was often fierce, but considerable effort had nevertheless often been made not to divide families terminally over the issue and respondents tended to have tried to patch up relations after their mothers' deaths. Views about the failure of formal services, however, were still strong:

> I think the anger and the bitterness that I have been left with is that the services just were there and I was not made aware of the help which was there, which would have added to mother's quality of life. I feel that not enough was done to help me. I wouldn't have needed very much, the things that could have been supplied without very much more expense. My overriding feeling is anger and bitterness . . . and the lack of co-ordination between the services and the unsympathetic approach and the

lack of understanding from professional people that you turn to thinking that they were there to help you and in fact you didn't get any help from them, they just made you feel worse with their attitudes.

This respondent thus summarized the major complaints respondents had about services, the lack of information, the lack of co-ordination, the gaps in provision, and the lack of sympathetic understanding experienced by many of them.

A large number said that they felt they had saved the state considerable amounts of money and that they deserved more sympathetic treatment. This feeling was also very strongly expressed in respect to the financial situation many found themselves in after their mothers' deaths. Two respondents found themselves considerably worse off when their mothers died because they lost access to their mothers' pensions. Others had forfeited income and pension rights by giving up work early or had not worked long enough to qualify for any reasonable occupational pension. A nurse had paid for contributions until she gave up work to care at age 55. Once her savings ran out she could not keep up the contributions and hence her pension was not index-linked and remained at its 1970 level: 'It was a big loss, a very big loss.' A majorty of carers felt a deep sense of injustice about becoming worse off themselves when saving the state money: 'I was always clobbered financially . . . it was a drain on my resources all the time.' Many respondents also reported their mothers being refused the attendance allowance at their first application, or only receiving the lower rate. Three were not informed of the existence of the allowance; one received it only after her mother died; and one was wrongly informed that her mother could not claim it while her daughter was working. One carer who had looked after both her parents all her adult life felt that she deserved a pension in her own right. She bitterly resented having to claim supplementary benefit:

It's not the same. It's not the same feeling to you inside here. I have worked for that and that's mine, but they're giving it to me under sufferance, which makes you feel you ought to have fallen off the earth sometimes, now they're gone and your useful life's over. It's that feeling of independence. Everybody needs it. Everybody needs to have a worth, to be worth something.

This statement reveals first, a dislike that may be associated more with the attitudes of an older generation of having to accept state benefits and second, a more general feeling that the work of caring tends to go largely unrecognized. A majority of carers felt that neither siblings, employers, the state, nor indeed the medical profession had much idea as to the day-to-day meaning of caring, or any great appreciation of the work that was being done. The lack of financial reward was only the most concrete manifestation of the lack of recognition generally accorded to carers.

Not surprisingly, many carers harboured fears and anxieties regarding their own ageing. Several had developed illnesses, or felt that health problems had been exacerbated by caring. Three had back problems, two had developed severe allergies during the period of caring and one diabetes, and several suffered from chronic insomnia. This was in addition to the nine who experienced some sort of breakdown during or after caring. With the image of their mothers' deteriorating health before them, many respondents had all too clear a picture of what they might experience themselves. Some who had cared for mothers with Alzheimer's Disease expressed fears that they might develop it themselves: 'I watch myself very closely and I see lots of signs, yes . . . there's a possibility that it's inherited.' And: 'What frightens me is to be *out of control* and to be subject to all these ghastly people. . . . ' One spoke more generally about the shock of feeling her own age when her mother died.

> I got what the French call a 'coup de vieux'. I suddenly realized how old I was. Because I was now the oldest person in the family. It was as if a great wall that had been feet away from you moved forward and you were only a foot from it.

These two respondents seem to have been especially protective of their mothers because of their own fears about ageing and their horror at the way in which they felt society at large treats elderly people. One woman felt strongly that as an ex-carer she was fighting a particular stereotype. She noted that no one had suggested that she do something for herself or even enjoy herself now that a long period of caring was over and felt that this was because society assumed elderly women's expectations to be small: 'I've got to fight people's attitude to me. I don't think my life's finished, hopefully it's just started.'

CARERS' PREFERENCES FOR THEIR OWN CARE

We had hoped to ask carers about their own preferences for care. In fact, very few were prepared to give any detailed thought to this question. As one put it: 'Oh I haven't thought about it yet. Not really, no. I'll just make the most of what's left until I *feel* old . . . sometimes my bones feel old enough though, but my mind doesn't.' Another was typical in hoping that she would not prove to be a burden to anyone,

> but you don't know do you? How can you prepare for old age, you can't really can you? You must wait for it to creep up on you. And then you hope that there by the grace of God . . . . Still . . . no point worrying about it, is there?

The majority had very little to say about their plans for the future. Three stated firmly that it was impossible to plan because it was impossible to predict their state of health: 'Wait and see' was the most common comment. One woman had a simple faith in the abstract web of reciprocity. While not religious, she felt strongly that: 'If you do what you can, when the time comes someone will come to your rescue.' She took great comfort from this and refused either to worry or think about the future. If pressed on this subject, most mentioned sheltered housing as being a good idea; three were already living in such accommodation. Only one, perhaps significantly the oldest respondent at 75 years, had made detailed plans for the future and investigated various old people's homes. Another, who was being cared for by a cousin and her husband whom she had invited to come and live with her, experienced constant frustration at not being able to obtain the sort of domiciliary care she needed. She was having considerable difficulty, despite her knowledge as an ex-carer, in getting the aids she needed. Confined to a wheelchair, she knew what she needed and knew it was available, but was unable to obtain appropriate help. Another woman who had cared for both parents for all her adult life and who was now experiencing considerable loneliness, was finding that there were particular tasks she could not perform, for instance changing light bulbs and dusting the tops of cupboards. However she had been told that this was not the sort of work a home help would do and she was resigned to soldiering on alone:

I said [to the home help supervisor] there's the majority of us that you want to keep active, but if you won't come in and do those sorts of things . . . they sit and talk to you as if you're a half wit. It doesn't mean to say that if your legs don't work you're a half wit. No thank you.

Consideration of their own futures forced carers to consider issues that were painful. Clare Wenger's (1984) research on the informal care networks of the elderly found that her sample expressed strong preferences for family care. However, West, Ill-sey, and Kelman's (1984) investigation of the care preferences of a random sample of the population in three Scottish areas showed only a limited preference for informal care without pro-fessional involvement. The position of ex-carers is additionally complicated. Our respondents had assumed responsibility for their mothers in addition to general household responsibilities, and had often become more assertive and independent as a result. Furthermore, having decided that their mothers should not go into a home, most were understandably reluctant to con-sider that option for themselves: 'I dread the thought of going into a home.' The single women knew that there would be no one to care for them: 'It's very different when you're on your own [nervous laugh]. I don't think about it to be honest – depress-ing.' Another remembered her mother having worried about 'who would look after the daughters'. One, whose mother had entered a home two years previously and was still alive, said that she would not mind a similar arrangement for herself, but her extreme hesitancy reflected her own profoundly ambivalent feel-ings about her decision respecting her mother, as well as her own desire to remain independent: 'It's very [pause] I don't, I mean, I think the home where my mother is does provide, I mean per-sonally, I've always thought I wouldn't mind communal care.'
Even if there was someone available to care for them in their turn, having told the interviewer about the problems of caring, it was almost impossible for respondents to say that they expected that person to do the same for them: 'I don't think one can think too much about it. I've got two god-daughters and I've always said I don't want anyone to look after me. Of course they wouldn't.' Married women with daughters of their own usually expressed doubts as to whether they would care. One woman whose son and daughter had been alienated during the period of

caring said of her daughter: 'I hope she would feel she could [care], but I hope I don't ever have to put her in that position. It'll take a long time for the reaction to grandma to wear off.' Another reported that: 'My daughter turned around to me in a joke, she said, "Don't think you're going to come here and live with me because you're not," she said, "we'll put you in a home with Nan." I wouldn't ever put myself on my daughter knowingly. . . . ' Yet another said simply: 'I wouldn't expect my child to care for me like I cared for my mother.' While these carers often harboured some hope that their daughters would in fact feel able to care, they knew only too well what they were asking and also appreciated that the lives their daughters led might be very different. For example, two said that if their daughters found themselves without supportive husbands it would prove impossible for them to care. Several said that siblings and other kin should help, or even share the care of an elderly person, but none contemplated a son assuming full responsibility for caring: 'I wouldn't ask them. And I've only got sons, I've got no daughters . . . it's not fair for boys. Don't ask me why but . . . I think the thing is that a girl is usually closer to her mum than men are.'

When asked about the merits of family care in the abstract, the answers were less tentative, but still remarkably ambivalent. Only one respondent felt unequivocally that daughters should care. A majority started their replies in the affirmative, but then went on to give what was often a long list of qualifications: 'Oh, yes, I certainly think . . . but I don't think that daughters should be expected to give up all their work and life to caring for people. . . . ' Others mentioned the importance of the daughter receiving proper help if she took on the responsibility of caring. But the majority stressed above all the importance of first, the daughter *wanting* to care, and second, of a good relationship between the mother and daughter before caring began: 'I think if they want to yes, if they don't want to no, because I mean you'd end up [pause] killing them or choking them. . . . ' And: 'With always the proviso that you want to do it, I think if a daughter or anybody else is forced to do it through circumstances . . . it can't do either of you any good really . . . but if you've got a good relationship then you're the obvious one to do it.' All the women we interviewed clearly felt some sense of family obligation to care which was revealed in their immediate reaction that in general

daughters should care. Yet several stated explicitly in the course
of qualifying their initial response that caring should not be
undertaken solely out of a sense of duty. The carefulness and
ambivalence of the replies to the question asking about the per-
petuation of this system of informal care is symptomatic of the
complex meaning of caring as part labour and part love, part
affection and part duty. The most frequent qualification articulated by respondents was that the carer must be friendly and
sympathetic towards the elderly person. Given that she met this
requirement, a daughter was preferred because she could additionally be expected to have more long-term commitment to a
parent.

Thus in their responses to questions about the future of family
care, respondents clearly gave priority to the importance of the
quality of the central caring relationship in any 'successful'caring
experience. The fact remains that all but three respondents
expressed some positive feelings about having cared, despite, in
many cases, a heavy burden or long period of care, painful deterioration of their relationships with the mothers, and lack of
external support. A majority expressed a sense of achievement
that their mothers did not have to leave home: 'It's a great comfort after they have died to know that you've done it and they
died in their own home.' Such comments revealed the carer's
sense of personal satisfaction at having coped and having succeeded in fulfilling her mother's wishes. In cases where the carer
felt considerable residual bitterness, especially about lost opportunities, or where the relationship between mother and daughter
had been exceptionally problematic, there was less likely to be a
sense of personal fulfilment, but there was still some pride in
having done the best possible, and considerable peace of mind: 'I
was surprised at what I actually coped with. [Satisfaction?] No,
peace of mind. I was with her actually the night she died.' Even
in cases where the caring experience had been extremely difficult
in all its aspects, and where the carer also felt considerable
bitterness and/or guilt (often about her behaviour towards her
mother or about the fact that her mother had in the end entered a
home), all but a very few still felt positively about having done
'the right thing': 'I don't think there was anything enjoyable
about it. Maybe I'm not the right type [laughs] . . . a little
satisfaction in knowing that you'd done the right thing.'

CHAPTER 9

Conclusions

It would be hard to overestimate the emotional and material costs of caring revealed by the caring biographies of our respondents. The investment in caring as both labour and love has a profound impact on the whole fabric of the carer's life and only in a minority of cases can the caring experience be described as a straightforwardly loving and balanced family relationship involving personal care. In other words, the giving of care necessarily involved more than the work of tending. It required psychological adjustment to the elderly person's deteriorating condition and to the changing quality of the relationship between carer and person cared for; it required careful balancing to maintain the other aspects of the carer's life which she considered important; and it required energy, determination, and emotional fortitude to enlist aid from external sources. Nevertheless, carers may suffer complete breakdown during or after caring and still be glad they cared.

The great majority of our carers wanted to care and would do so over again, even with the benefit of hindsight; although only a minority said they would do as much for as long for someone other than their mothers, indeed only five could be described as 'vocation carers', going on to care for other kin, neighbours, or friends. The injunction to care is extremely powerful and must be related not only, in the case of this study, to the special feelings of affection and obligation that may be engendered by the relationship between mother and daughter, but also to the personal sense of satisfaction and identity that accrues to the carer. In part the latter are derived from societal pressures; women grow up expecting to care for children, husbands, and kin, and are expected to put caring before other commitments. One respondent was subjected to severe pressure from friends of her mother and from neighbours to give up work and care for her mother full-time: 'Even the day she died, coming home from work, I saw a friend of hers, who by the time I got off the bus had convinced me that I hadn't done all that I should.' Those whose only posit-ive feeling about caring was that they had done 'the right thing' were bowing to this considerable social pressure on women to care.

The injunction to care was clearly internalized and may indeed be part of the feminine identity: 'The ideal of care is thus an activ-ity of relationship, of seeing and responding to need, taking care of the world by sustaining the web of connection so that no one is left alone' (Gilligan 1982: 62). Gilligan stresses the self-sacrificing elements that emanate from the ethic of care, but the web of inti-macy and relationship is also self-serving in so far as women depend on it and manipulate it. It may be argued that because the feminine personality comes to define itself in relation to others rather than by a process of separation, women have little choice but to depend on the connections they have with other people, and, if Gilligan is right, a woman's identity will be entwined with that of others. Nevertheless, women do derive considerable security from the private world of relationships they have constructed, nor does it necessarily follow that women will inevitably silence their own voices because of the fear of hurting others. They may also manoeuvre within relationships, playing off one actor against another – a friend against a sister in the case of the carer who felt very resentful about her sister's lack of help – and take active steps to shift the balance of relationships between friends and neighbours for example, or between them-selves and their mothers. Thus while caring should be seen as part of the construction of femininity, women do not necessarily experience caring as either a matter of self-sacrifice or of power-lessness. Positive feelings about caring are often derived not only from abstract satisfaction at obeying the injunction to care, but from the reality of the caring experience, and in particular from the companionship, emotional security, and appreciation it brings the carer. It is significant that when asked generally about the merits of family care, our respondents identified the quality of the relationship between a prospective carer and person cared for as the most important factor to be considered in any decision to care.

Our interviews revealed instances of considerable self-sacrifice on the part of some carers, and in some circumstances there is little doubt that despite some sense of satisfaction, caring can be destructive of self and harmful to physical health and welfare. Furthermore, the research reveals that there are some clear signals as to when this is likely to become the case. A carer who immerses herself in caring to the exclusion of other activities and relationships; who receives little support from kin, friends, neighbours, employers, or professionals; who finds the nature of the caring tasks she is presented with particularly difficult to deal with either psychologically or physically; whose relationship with the person cared for is problematic; or who is struggling to identify herself with some project other than caring, is likely to be 'at risk'. In particular, it seems that professional helpers tend to miss the problems experienced by those who immerse themselves in caring, doubtless because these women appear to be committed to caring and to be 'coping'. It is sometimes assumed that caring will be much easier if carer and person cared for have always lived together and the carer either sees caring as a 'natural' development or 'drifts' into it (for example, Harris 1984). However, our research indicates that this is only one of many factors in what we have called the caring matrix that determine the nature of the caring experience. While the length of the period of co-residence and reasons for co-residence seem to be important predictors of the responses to caring – those making a conscious decision to live with and care for their mothers being much more likely to be 'balancers' – no one response necessarily ensures a positive or negative caring experience. The most important factor determining how the carer feels about caring would appear to be the quality of the primary caring relationship, but this must be considered in relation to both the carer's other priorities and relationships, and the sources of support.

Just as the meaning of caring is complex and involves the understanding of a whole set of relationships and circumstances which must be understood as the cumulative effects of the individual's caring biography, so it is unlikely that there will be any one simple solution to the problem of supporting the supporters. While the majority of our respondents wanted to care, they also often felt that their experiences could have been significantly improved if more help had been forthcoming, and while many would have preferred additional informal or voluntary help, we would argue that the professional helper is in a position to play a make or break role in assisting carers. This is not to deny or demean the support provided by kin, friends, and neighbours. However, our research indicated that a principal carer is identified early, usually before the period of co-resident care begins, even though we did not set out to examine this process in detail. Once the pattern of co-resident care is established, the principal carer assumes full responsibility for the dependant. Kin and networks of friends and neighbours can play a vital role, especially in sustaining the carer's morale, but their contribution to the performance of the caring tasks is strictly limited. Furthermore, their contribution tends to decrease as the condition of the person cared for deteriorates and the intensity of the primary caring relationship increases. It is in this situation that the assistance of professional helpers becomes crucial, although we would suggest that offers of professional help should not be withheld until such time as other sources of support have fallen away. Professional intervention before this stage, even when there is a spouse or other family help, can do much to ease the burden of caring. However, such assistance can only be effective if the helper is sensitive to the meaning of caring and reaches some understanding of the carer's attitudes and circumstances, including the continuing, if limited, involvement of significant others.

In particular we would draw attention to the importance of understanding both the possible length, nature, and dimensions of the caring experience. The full extent of the caring sequence was revealed only because of our decision to collect caring biographies rather than undertake a 'snapshot' study of carers' needs or relationships. At some point, all but four of our respondents became full-time carers, but prior to this most experienced a period of what we have called semi-care and of part-time full care. Four experienced extremely long periods of semi-care, amounting to thirty-three years in one case. At each stage in the sequence, which is not necessarily progressive, the carer needs different kinds of support, relating not just to the stages in the illness of the person cared for, but also to the stress the carer may experience as a result of the effects of caring on her relationships with friends, kin, or an employer. A long period of semi-care merits more recognition as a source of strain for carers. During this period and during the more intensive period of part-time full care, the carer is trying to balance her caring responsibilities with other aspects of her extra-caring life.

It is possible that during the period of full care, when the balance of the carer's concerns is shifted from paid work or caring for other family members to caring for the elderly dependant, the carer's physical burden may be eased by increasing professional support. However, the evidence suggests that such support may not always be either entirely appropriate or sympathetic. During this stage of co-resident care, carers are liable to become isolated and increasingly immersed in caring and are therefore especially in need of emotional support. The need for emotional support and counselling is also particularly pronounced when co-resident care ends. As we discussed in the last chapter, the majority of our respondents reported considerable difficulty in picking up the pieces when their mothers died, or in coming to terms with admitting their mothers to an institution. Additionally, some experienced difficulty in coming to terms with their own ageing. We would argue that the normal emotions experienced in relation to bereavement and ageing were intensified for our respondents because of their experience of caring. In a society which relies on people to take on this role, partly to relieve pressure on publicly funded services, 'support for the supporters' must include help for carers in the aftermath of the caring process.

Professional supporters may encounter carers and persons cared for during any phase of the caring sequence. In our view an understanding of the possible dimensions of the caring sequence is important for helpers, because what might constitute a suitable intervention at one stage may be completely inappropriate at another. During the semi-care period, for instance, the person cared for may well be in routine, infrequent contact with a professional worker such as a GP or district nurse. At this stage, it is unlikely that much in the way of information or practical or emotional support is required by the carer. As caring continues, different kinds of support may become needed and an offer which may have been turned down at an early stage, such as day care, may become appropriate, indeed essential. Understanding of the stage that has been reached in caring and of the duration of this and previous stages of caring, is a prerequisite for determining appropriate mixes of help.

We conceptualized the non-temporal dimensions of caring as a set of relationships and circumstances which we called the caring matrix. Working outwards from the primary caring relationship, the caring matrix enables an appreciation of the way in which the balance of relationships within the matrix changes during the caring period. If crucial elements of the matrix are missing – such as supportive relationships with friends, neighbours, and kin – or the balance of the matrix is distorted by, for instance, the mother moving house or the daughter giving up work, the need for professional support becomes greater. The extra-caring relationships of both the carer and person cared for are almost certain to be progressively narrowed after the establishment of the co-resident caring relationships. The matrix focuses attention on the primary caring relationship and the way in which the carer and person cared for experience caring. It thus provides the potential helper with a set of reference points that relate directly to the caring situation rather than to the particular disciplinary preoccupations of the helper, and it may therefore provide a more realistic and useful guide for assessing the carer's needs. At present it seems that there is, on the one hand, a tendency for professional helpers to pay insufficient attention to the demands generated by carers' extra-caring lives and therefore to offer inappropriate support; and on the other hand to fail to recognize that carers may not always articulate their needs. Some do not ask for help because they feel that they can, or should be able to, cope, while others do not recognize the stress imposed on them by the caring routine until it is too late.

Together, the concept of the caring sequence and the caring matrix seek to isolate what the caring experiences we studied had in common, and thereby to provide a framework within which caring may be located and understood. The strength of informal caring is the uniquely individual pattern of care it is able to provide, but it is this that also makes it so difficult to devise systems of support for the supporters. Our approach has been to explore empirically recent insights into the meaning of caring as both labour and love, emphasizing the importance of recognizing caring as an ever-changing set of relationships and of developing both a rather different way of looking at, and a new vocabulary for talking about, caring.

We hope that this will serve to open up discussion, first across professional boundaries. The role of supporter is a difficult one for professional helpers to develop. The relationship between professional and informal carer is not the usual one of client and professional; the professional helper must work out how to supplement rather than direct. Also, because caring is a mixture of labour and love, care in an informal setting may become contested territory: some of our respondents wanted a particular form of support, but were nevertheless convinced that they knew what was best for their mothers, or because of their pride in and identification with the role of carer, experienced great difficulty in asking for help.

In fact, the relationship between carers and professional helpers is often conceptualized as a linear one (for example, Naut and Schuyt 1985). This may serve to perpetuate a rather narrow approach whereby the professional does not intervene until the resources of the carer and informal helpers are virtually exhausted. The professional helper then tends to focus on a particular aspect of need determined by his or her own discipline rather than the reality of the complex set of caring relationships, and may tend to displace the carer rather than supplement her work. Most of our respondents wanted to know that help was available if they needed it. They did not necessarily want a particular aspect of care taken over by professionals, rather they wanted practical or emotional help and support to supplement the work they were already doing, and to relieve the weight of a growing physical or mental burden. The caring matrix refocuses attention on the perceptions of the carer and person cared for and thereby provides a surer guide to the different situations that require a variety of kinds of support.

Second, a caring-relationship-centred perspective also opens up the discussion about the relationship between informal and formal care. Recent government policy documents have tended to view informal and formal care systems as alternatives, implying that the former should in large part replace the latter. Our evidence suggests that carers do want to care, but that they also need considerable support to enable them to do so. Thus, to try and increase the caring done informally at the expense of formal provision will not do. There is, in any case, no evidence to show that participation by the informal sector can be greatly increased (Walker 1985).

But if the two systems of care cannot be seen as alternatives, it remains to suggest a more realistic conceptualization of the relationship between them. Some writers have argued in favour of a partnership, or the 'interweaving' of formal or informal care, but as Pinker (1985) has cautioned, the systems are separate. Informal systems operate on different principles from formal ones. Given our finding that despite the costs the women in our sample wanted to care, and our conceptualization of caring as a set of relationships whose balance shifts over time, the most successful approach may be for professional helpers in the formal sector to recognize the centrality of the primary caring relationship and to work to respond to and support it. The informal and formal systems cannot be seen as points on a continuum, as they are in a linear model. In a co-resident care situation, the informal system predominates and it falls to the professional to adopt a caring-relationship-centred perspective and to work to 'fill the gaps'. When the dependant enters an institution, the formal system predominates. It then falls to informal carers to fill the gaps. This means that professionals must appreciate the period of institutionalization as part of the caring sequence and recognize the residual power of the primary caring relationship. In other words, an appreciation of the caring biography provides the basis for the reservation of a role for informal carers even in formal settings.

In the final analysis there is no doubt but that this sort of approach is more likely to become a reality in what Walker (1985) has described as a 'caring society', where caring is recognized and valued and where more men share the care both in the private and the public spheres. But in the meantime, it is not unreasonable to suggest that helpers adopt a more caring-relationship-centred perspective.

References

The References section includes works referred to in the text. The Resource bibliography (p.167) includes other material which we used in developing our idea of caring as a matrix of relationships and indicates the range of interdisciplinary material we relied on in developing our semi-structured interview schedules.

Abrams, P. (1984) 'Evaluating soft findings: some problems of measuring informal care', *Journal of Social Services Research Group* 2, 1–8.

Allan, Graham (1983) 'Informal networks of care: issues raised by Barclay', *Journal of Social Work* 13, 417–33.

Allan, Graham (1984) 'Friendship and care for elderly people', *Ageing and Society* 6, 1.

Allen, Isobel; with Levin, Enid; Sidell, Moyra; and Vetter, Norman (1983) 'The elderly and their informal carers', in DHSS, *Elderly People in the Community: Their Service Needs. Research Contributions to the Development of Policy and Practice.*

Anderson, Michael (1971) *Family Structure in Nineteenth Century Lancashire*, Cambridge: Cambridge University Press.

Arber, Sarah; Evandrou, Maria; Gilbert, Nigel; and Dale, Angela (1986) 'Gender, household composition and receipt of domiciliary services by the elderly disabled', paper presented at British Sociological Association Annual Conference, Loughborough: University of Loughborough.

Atkinson, A.B. (1984) *Poverty in Britain: the 1930s to the 1980s*, ESRC Programme no. 73, London: HMSO.

Audit Commission (1985) *Managing Social Services for the Elderly More Effectively*, London: HMSO.

Audit Commission (1986) *Making a Reality of Community Care*, London: Audit Commission for Local Authorities in England and Wales.

Ayer, S. and Alaszewski A. (1984) *Community Care and the Mentally Handicapped*, London: Croom Helm.

Bayley, M (1973) *Mental Handicap and Community Care: a Study of Mentally Handicapped People in Sheffield*, London: Routledge & Kegan Paul.

Bean, Phillip; Ferris, John; and Whynes, David (1985) *In Defence of Welfare*, London: Tavistock.

de Beauvoir, Simone (1966) *A Very Easy Death*, London: Weidenfeld & Nicolson.

Bengston, Vern L. *et al*. (1985) 'Generations, cohorts and relations between age groups', in R. Binstock and E. Shanas (eds), *Handbook of Aging and the Social Sciences*, 304–32.

Bengston, Vern L. and Troll, Lillian (1978) 'Youth and their parents: feedback and intergenerational influence on socialization', in Richard M. Lerner and Graham B. Spanier (eds), *Child Influences on Marital and Family Interaction*, 215–40.

Binstock, R. and Shanas, E. (eds) (1985) *Handbook of Aging and the Social Sciences*, 2nd edn, New York: Van Nostrand Reinholt Co.

Blau, Zena Smith (1973) *Old Age in a Changing Society*, New York: New Viewpoints.

Briggs, Anna and Oliver, Judith (1985) *Caring. Experiences of Looking After Disabled Relatives*, London: Routledge & Kegan Paul.

Brody, Elaine M. (1981) ' "Women in the middle" and family help to older people', *The Gerontologist* 21, 471–80.

Brody, Elaine M.; Johnson, Pauline T.; Fulcomer, Mark C.; and Lang, Abigail M. (1983) 'Women's changing roles and help to elderly parents: attitudes of three generations of women', *Journal of Gerontology* 38, 597–607.

Brody, Elaine M. and Schoonover, Claire B. (1986) 'Patterns of parentcare when adult daughters work and when they do not', *The Gerontologist* 26, 372–81.

Bromberg, Eleanor Mallach (1983) 'Mother–daughter relationships in later life: the effect of quality of relationship upon mutual aid', *Journal of Gerontological Social Work* 6, 75–92.

Brubaker, Timothy H. (ed.) (1983) *Family Relationships in Later Life*, Beverly Hills: Sage.

Bulmer, Martin (1986a) *Neighbours. The Work of Philip Abrams*, Cambridge: Cambridge University Press.

Bulmer, Martin (1986b) 'Can caring come together?' *New Society*, 4 July, 18–20.

Bytheway, W.R. and Gilligan, J.H. (1984) *Caring for the Carer: When the Carer Retires*, Occasional Paper no. 5, Swansea: University College School of Social Studies.

Cheal, David J. (1983) 'Intergenerational family transfers', *Journal of Marriage and the Family* 45, 805–13.

Chodorow, Nancy (1978) *The Reproduction of Mothering: Psychoanalysis and the Sociology of Gender*. Berkeley: University of California Press.

Cicirelli, Victor G. (1983) 'Adult children and their elderly parents', in Timothy H. Brubaker (ed.), *Family Relationships in Later Life*.

Dalley, Gillian (1988) *Ideologies of Caring: Rethinking Community and Collectivism*, London: Macmillan.

Davey, Audrey (1984) 'The experience of caring', in W.R. Bytheway and J.H. Gilligan (eds) *Caring for the Carer: When the Carer Retires*.

Deimling, G.T. and Poulshock, S.W. (1985) 'The transition from family in-home care to institutional care', *Research on Ageing* 7, 563–76.

DHSS and Welsh Office (1978) *A Happier Old Age*, London: HMSO.

DHSS (1983) *Elderly People in the Community: Their Service Needs. Research Contributions to the Development of Policy and Practice*, London: HMSO.

Ducquenin, Anthea (1984) 'Who doesn't marry and why', *Oral History* 12.

Elshtain, J.B. (1981) *Public Man and Private Woman*, Oxford: Blackwell.

EOC (1982a) *Caring for the Elderly and Handicapped: Community Care Policies and Women's Lives*, Manchester: Equal Opportunities Commission.

EOC (1982b) *Who Cares for the Carers?* Manchester: Equal Opportunities Commission.

Ermisch, John (1983) *The Political Economy of Demographic Change*, London: Heinemann.

Evandrou, M.; Arber, S.; Dale, A.; and Gilbert, G.N. (1986) 'Who cares for the elderly? Family care provision and receipt of statutory services', in C. Phillipson, M. Bernard, and P. Straug (eds), *Dependency and Independence in Old Age: Theoretical Perspectives and Policy Alternatives*, London: British Society of Gerontology.

Evers, Helen (1983) 'Elderly women and disadvantage: perceptions of daily life and support relationships', in Dorothy Jerrome (ed.), *Ageing in Modern Society*.

Evers, Helen (1984) 'Old women's self perceptions of dependency and some implications for service provision', *Journal of Epidemiology and Community Health* 38, 306–9.

Evers, Helen (1985) 'The frail elderly woman: emergent questions in ageing and women's health', in Ellen Lewin and Virginia Olesen (eds) *Women, Health and Healing*.

Fengler, Alfred P. and Goodrich, Nancy (1979) 'Wives of elderly disabled men: the hidden patients', *The Gerontologist* 19, 175–83.

Fennel, Graham; Phillipson, Chris; and Wenger, Clare (1983) 'The process of ageing: social aspects', in DHSS, *Elderly People in the Community: Their Service Needs. Research Contributions to the Development of Policy and Practice*.

Finch, Janet, and Groves, Dulcie (eds) (1983) *A Labour of Love: Women, Work and Caring*, London: Routledge & Kegan Paul.

Fisher, Lucy Rose (1986) *Linked Lives. Adult Daughters and their Mothers*, New York: Harper & Row.

Firth, Raymond; Hubert, Jane; and Forge, Anthony (1969) *Families and their Relatives*, London: Routledge & Kegan Paul.

Gilligan, Carol (1982) *In a Different Voice. Psychological Theory and Women's Development*, Cambridge, Mass.: Harvard University Press.

Glendinning, Caroline (1983) *Unshared Care. Parents and their Disabled Children*, London: Routledge & Kegan Paul.

Goldberg, E.M. and Hatch, Stephen (1981) *A New Look at the Personal Social Services*, Discussion Paper no. 4, London: Policy Studies Institute.

Goldberg, E.M. and Connelly, Naomi (1982) *The Effectiveness of Social Care for the Elderly. An Overview of Recent and Current Evaluative Research*, London: Heinemann.

Graham, Hilary (1983) 'Caring: a labour of love', in Janet Finch and Dulcie Groves (eds), *A Labour of Love: Women, Work and Caring*.

Hareven, Tamara K. (1982) *Family Time and Industrial Time*, Cambridge: Cambridge University Press.

Hareven, Tamara K. and Adams, Kathleen J. (eds) (1982) *Ageing and Life Course Transitions: an Interdisciplinary Perspective*, London: Tavistock.

Harper, Sarah, and Thane, Pat (1986) 'The contribution of the retirement debate to the social construct of old age in post-War Britain 1945–65', paper given at ESRC Initiative on Ageing Workshop, University of Surrey. To be published by Tavistock in a collection edited by Margot Jefferys.

Harris, C.C. (1984) 'A sociological perspective on ageing within families', in W.R. Bytheway and J.H. Gilligan, *Caring for the Carer: When the Carer Retires*.

Harrison, Jo (1983) 'Women and ageing: experience and implications', *Ageing and Society* 3, 209–35.

Hatch, Stephen (1983) *Volunteers: Patterns, Meanings and Motives*, Berkhamstead: The Volunteer Centre.

Havighurst, Robert J.; Neugarten, Bernice L.; and Tobin, Sheldon S. (1968) 'Disengagement and patterns of ageing', in Bernice L. Neugarten (ed.), *Middle Age and Aging*.

Hawley, P. and Chamley, J.D. (1986) 'Older persons' perceptions of the quality of their human support systems', *Ageing and Society* 6, 295–312.

Hess, Beth B. and Waring, Joan M. (1978) 'Parent and child in later life: rethinking the relationship', in Richard M. Lerner and Graham B. Spanier (eds), *Child Influences on Marital and Family Interaction*, 241–73.

Hess, Beth B. and Waring, Joan M (1983) 'Family relationships of older women: a women's issue', in Elizabeth W. Markson, *Old Women. Issues and Prospects*.

Holter, Harriet (ed.) (1984) *Patriarchy in a Welfare State*, Bergen: University of Bergen Press.

Hooyman, N. and Lustbader, W. (1986) *Taking Care. Supporting Older People and their Families*, New York: Free Press.

Hunt, Audrey (1978) *The Elderly at Home,* London: HMSO.

Isaacs, Bernard; Livingstone, Maureen; and Neville, Yvonne (1972) *Survival of the Unfittest,* London: Routledge & Kegan Paul.

Jerrome, Dorothy (ed.) (1983) *Ageing in Modern Society,* London: Croom Helm.

Johnson, Malcolm L. (1978) 'Biographies and the assessment of needs in older people'. Paper given at the World Congress of Sociology, Uppsala, Sweden.

Jones, Dee A.; Victor, Christina R.; and Vetter, Norman J. (1983) 'Carers of the elderly in the community', *Journal of the Royal College of General Practitioners* 33, 707–10.

Joshi, Heather (1984) *Women's Participation in Paid Work,* Dept of Employment Research Paper no. 45, London: Department of Employment.

Kline, Chrysee (1975) 'The socialization process of women: implications for a theory of successful aging', *The Gerontologist,* 15, 486–92.

Koshberg, J.I. and Cairl, R.E. (1986) 'The cost of care index: a case management tool for screening informal care providers', *The Gerontologist* 26, 273–9.

Land, H. and Rose, H. (1985) 'Compulsory altruism for some or an altruistic society for all?' in Philip Bean, John Ferris, and David Whynes, *In Defence of Welfare.*

Lerner, Richard M. and Spanier, Graham B. (eds) (1978) *Child Influences on Marital and Family Interaction,* New York: Academic Press.

Levin, Enid; Sinclair, Ian; and Gorbach, Peter (1983) *The Supporters of Confused Elderly Persons at Home,* London: National Institute of Social Work.

Lewin, Ellen and Olesen, Virginia (eds) (1985) *Women, Health and Healing,* London: Tavistock.

Lewis, Jane (1986) *What Price Community Medicine?* Brighton: Wheatsheaf.

Lewis, Jane; Porter, Marilyn; and Shrimpton, Mark (eds) (1988) *Women, Work and Family in the British, Canadian and Norwegian Offshore Oil Industry,* London: Macmillan.

Litwak, E (1985) *Helping the Elderly. The Complementary Roles of Informal Networks and Formal Systems,* New York: Guilford Press.

Markson, Elizabeth (1983) *Older Women. Issues and Prospects,* Lexington, Mass.: Lexington Books.

Marsden, D. and Abrams, S. (1987) 'Allies, liberators, intruders and cuckoos in the nest: towards a sociology of caring over the life cycle', in T. Keil *et al.* (eds) *Women and the Life Cycle,* BSA Conference, vol. II. London: Macmillan.

Martin, J. David (1971) 'Power and dependence and the complaints of the elderly: a social exchange perspective', *Ageing and Human Development* 2, 106–12.

Martin, Jean and Roberts, Ceridwen (1984) *Women and Employment. A*

Lifetime Perspective, London: HMSO.

Matthews, Sarah H. (1979) *The Social World of Old Women*, Beverly Hills: Sage Library of Social Research no. 78.

Means, R. and Smith, R. (1985) *The Development of Welfare Services for Elderly People*, London: Croom Helm.

Moroney, R.M. (1976) *The Family and the State: Considerations for Social Policy*, London: Longmans.

Naut, J. and Schuyt, T. (1985) 'Mediating structures and the exchange of social care and individual responsibility', in J.A. Yoder, J.M.L. Jonker, R.A.B. Leaper (eds), *Support Networks in a Caring Community*.

Neisser, E.G. (1973) *Mothers and Daughters. A Lifelong Relationship*. New York: Harper and Row.

Neugarten, Bernice L. (ed.) (1968) *Middle Age and Aging. A Reader in Social Psychology*, Chicago: University of Chicago Press.

Nissel, M. and Bonnerjea, L. (1982) *Family Care of the Handicapped Elderly: who pays?* Report no. 602, London: PSI.

Parliamentary Papers (1981) DHSS, Sec. of State for Scotland, Northern Ireland and Wales, *Growing Older*, Cmnd. 8173, London: HMSO.

Parker, Roy (1981) 'Tending and social policy', in E. Matilda Goldberg and Stephen Hatch, *A New Look at the Personal Social Services*.

Pateman, Carole (1979) *The Problem of Political Obligation*, New York: John Wiley.

Phillipson, C. (1982) *Capitalism and the Construction of Old Age*, London: Macmillan.

Pinker, R.A. (1985) 'Social policy and social care: divisions of responsibility', in J.A. Yoder, J.M.L. Jonker, and R.A.B. Leaper, *Support Networks in a Caring Community*.

Plummer, Ken (1983) *Documents of Life. An Introduction to the Problems and Literature of a Humanistic Method*, London: Allen & Unwin.

Qureshi, Hazel; Challis, David; and Davies, Bleddyn (1983) 'Motivations and rewards of helpers in the Kent Community Care Scheme', in Stephen Hatch, *Volunteers: Patterns, Meanings and Motives*, 144–67.

Qureshi, Hazel and Walker, Alan (1988) *The Caring Relationship*, London: Routledge & Kegan Paul.

Robinson, Betsy and Thurnher, Majda (1979) 'Taking care of aged parents: a family life cycle transition', *The Gerontologist* 19, 586–93.

Rossiter, C. and Wicks, M. (1982) *Crisis or Challenge? Family Care, Elderly People and Social Policy*, Occasional Paper no. 8, London: Study Commission on the Family.

Rowntree, B. Seebohm (1947) *Old People*, Oxford: Nuffield Foundation, Oxford University Press.

Sheldon, Frances (1982) 'Supporting the supporters: working with the relatives of patients with dementia', *Age and Ageing* 11, 184–8.

Sheldon, J.H. (1948) *The Social Medicine of Old Age. Report of an Inquiry in Wolverhampton*, Oxford: Nuffield and Oxford University Press.

Smith, M. Dwayne and Self, George D. (1980) 'The congruence between mothers' and daughters' sex-role attitudes: a research note', *Journal of Marriage and the Family* 42, 105–9.

Taylor, Hedley (1983) *The Hospice Movement in Britain: its Role and Future*, London: Centre for Policy on Ageing.

Timaeus, Ian (1986) 'Families and households of the elderly population: prospects for those approaching old age', *Ageing and Society* 6, 271–93.

Townsend, Peter (1957) *The Family Life of Old People*, London: Routledge & Kegan Paul.

Troll, Lillian E.; Miller, Sheila J.; and Atchley, Robert C. (1979) *Families in Later Life*, Belmont Ca.: Wadsworth Publications.

Ungerson, C. (1985) 'Gender divisions and community care – a British perspective', paper given at ESRC-sponsored conference, University of Canterbury.

Waerness, K. (1984) 'Caregiving as women's work in the welfare state', in Harriet Holter (ed.), *Patriarchy in a Welfare Society*.

Walker, Alan (1983) 'Care for elderly people: a conflict between women and the state', in Janet Finch and Dulcie Groves (eds), *A Labour of Love: Women, Work and Caring*.

Walker, Alan (1985) 'From welfare state to caring society? The promise of informal support networks', in J.A. Yoder, J.M.L. Jonker, and R.A.B. Leaper (eds), *Support Networks in a Caring Community*.

Walker, Alan (1986) 'Community care: fact and fiction', in Alan Walker, Paul Ekblom, and Nicholas Deakin, *The Debate about Community: Papers from a Seminar on Community in Social Policy*, London: PSI.

Wall, R. (1984) 'Residential isolation of the elderly: a comparison over time', *Ageing and Society* 4, 483–503.

Wenger, C. (1984) *The Supportive Network: Coping with Old Age*, London: Allen & Unwin.

West, Patrick; Illsey, Raymond; and Kelman, Howard (1984) 'Public preferences for the care of dependency groups', *Social Science and Medicine* 18, 287–95.

Wicks, M. and Henwood, M. (1984) *The Forgotten Army: Family Care and Elderly People*, London: Family Policy Studies Centre.

Wilkin, David (1979) *Caring for the Mentally Handicapped Child*, London: Croom Helm.

Willmott, Peter (1986) *Social Networks. Informal Care and Public Policy*, Research Report 655, London: PSI.

Willmott, P. and Young, Michael (1960) *Family and Class in a London Suburb*, London: Routledge & Kegan Paul.

Wolfenden, Baron John (1978) *The Future of Voluntary Organisations. Report of the Wolfenden Committee*, London: Croom Helm.

Wright, Fay (1986) *Left Alone to Care*, London: Gower.

Yoder, J.A.; Jonker, J.M.L.; and Leaper, R.A.B. (eds) (1985) *Support Networks in a Caring Community*, Dordrecht: Martinus Nijhoff.

Resource bibliography

Age Concern (1975) *The Attitudes of the Retired and the Elderly*, London: Age Concern.

Albrecht, Stan L.; Bahr, Howard M.; and Chadwick, Bruce A. (1979) 'Changing family and sex roles: an assessment of age differences', *Journal of Marriage and the Family* 41, 41–50.

Allen, Isobel (1983) *Short-Stay Residential Care for the Elderly*, London: PSI.

Barker, Jonathan (1980) 'The relationship of "informal" care to "formal" social services: who helps people deal with social and health problems if they arise in old age?' in Susan Lonsdale, Adrian Webb, and Thomas L. Briggs (eds), *Teamwork in the Personal Social Services and Health Care*.

Baruch, Grace and Barnett, Rosalind C (1983) 'Adult daughters' relationships with their mothers', *Journal of Marriage and the Family* 45, 601–6.

Brearley, C. Paul (1977) *Residential Work with the Elderly*, London: Routledge & Kegan Paul.

Briggs, Anna (1983) *Who Cares? The Report of a Door to Door Survey into the Numbers and Needs of People Caring for Elderly Relatives*, London: Association of Carers.

Bromley, David B. (ed.) (1984) *Gerontology: Social and Behavioural Perspectives*, London: Croom Helm.

Brubaker, Timothy H. (1985) *Later Life Families*, Beverly Hills: Sage.

Burr, Wesley R.; Hill, Reuben; Nye, F. Ivan; and Reiss, Ira L. (eds) (1979) *Contemporary Theories about the Family*, vol. I, New York: Free Press.

Cantor, Marjorie H. (1983) 'Strain among caregivers: a study of experience in the US', *The Gerontologist* 23, 597–604.

Charlesworth, A; Within, D.; and Durie, A. (1984) *Carers and Services: a Comparison of Men and Women Caring for Dependent Elderly People*, Manchester: Equal Opportunities Commission.

Christenson, James A. (1977) 'Generational family differences', *The Gerontologist* 17, 367–71.

Cohler, Bertram J. and Grunebaum, Henry (1981) *Mothers, Grandmothers and Daughters*, New York: John Wiley.

Croft, Suzy (1986) 'Women, caring and the recasting of need – a feminist reappraisal', *Critical Social Policy* no. 16, 23–39.

Davis, Linda J (1980) 'Service provision and the elderly: attitudes of three generations of urban women', *The Occupational Therapy Journal of Research* 1, 32–52.

Dooghe, G. and Helander, J. (eds) (1979) *Family Life in Old Age*, The Hague: Martinus Nijhoff.

Dowd, James J. (1975) 'Aging as exchange: a preface to theory', *Journal of Gerontology* 30, 584–94.

Elder, Glen H. (1981) 'Historical experiences in the later years', in Tamara K. Hareven and Kathleen J. Adams (eds), *Ageing and Life Course Transitions: an Interdisciplinary Perspective*, 75–107.

Fengler, Alfred P.; Donigelis, Nicholas; and Little, Virginia C. (1983) 'Later life satisfaction and household structure: living with others and living alone', *Ageing and Society* 3, 357–77.

Firth, Raymond (1956) *Two Studies of Kinship in London*, London: Athlone Press.

Fogel, Robert W.; Hatfield, Elaine; Kiesler, Sara B.; and Shanas, Ethel (eds) (1981) *Aging, Stability and Change in the Family*, New York: Academic Press.

Frankfather, D.L.; Smith, M.J.; and Caro, Francis G. (1981) *Family Care of the Elderly*, Lexington, Mass.: D.C. Heath Co.

Glendenning, Frank (1982) *Care in the Community: Recent Research and Current Projects*, University of Keele: Beth Johnson Foundation Publications.

Hagestad, Gunhild O. (1981) 'Problems and promises in the social psychology of intergenerational relations', in Robert W. Fogel, Elaine Hatfield, Sara B. Kiesler, and Ethel Shanas (eds), *Aging, Stability and Change in the Family*.

Hammer, Signe (1975) *Daughters and Mothers. Mothers and Daughters*, New York Times Book Co.: Quadrangle.

Heinemann, Gloria D. (1983) 'Family involvement and support for widowed persons', in Timothy H. Brubaker (ed.), *Family Relationships in Later Life*.

Hellebrandt, Frances A. (1980) 'Ageing among the advantaged: a new look at the stereotype of the elderly', *The Gerontologist* 20, 404–17.

Hobman, David (ed.) (1978) *The Social Challenge of Ageing*, London: Croom Helm.

Hobman, David (ed.) (1981) *The Impact of Ageing. Strategies for Care*, London: Croom Helm.

Horowitz, Amy and Shindelman, Lois W. (1983) 'Reciprocity and affection: past influences on current caregiving', *Journal of Gerontological Social Work* 5, 5–20.

Itzin, C. (1984) 'The double jeopardy of ageism and sexism. Media images of women', in David B. Bromley, *Gerontology: Social and Behavioural Perspectives*.

Jerrome, Dorothy (1981) 'The significance of friendship for women in later-life', *Ageing and Society* 1, 175–97.

Johnson, Elizabeth S. (1978) 'Good relationships between older mothers and their daughters: a causal model', *The Gerontologist* 18, 301–6.

Johnson, Elizabeth S. (1981–2) 'Role expectations and role realities of older Italian mothers and their daughters', *International Journal of Aging and Human Development*, 14, 271–6.

Lesnoff-Caravaglia, G. (1983) *The World of Older Women*, New York: Human Science Press.

Lonsdale, Susan; Webb, Adrian; and Briggs, Thomas L. (eds) (1980) *Teamwork in the Personal Social Services and Health Care*, London: Personal Social Services Council and Croom Helm.

McEwen, Evelyn (1980) *Family Care of the Elderly. A Study in Personal Social Services and Housing Policy since the Second World War*, MSc Dissertation, London School of Economics.

Maddox, George L.; Siegler, I.C.; and Blazer, D.G. (1980) *Families and Older Persons: Policy Research and Practice*, Duke University Centre for Study of Ageing and Human Development.

Marris, P. (1958) *Widows and their Families*, London: Routledge & Kegan Paul.

Mellor, Hugh W. (1981) 'Family and other non-statutory care', in R.F.A. Shegog, *The Impending Crisis of Old Age: A Challenge to Ingenuity*.

Michaud, Ellen (1985) 'The story of Miss P', *New Society*, 6 December, 410–11.

National Council for the Single Woman and Her Dependants (1971) *The Single Woman: Keeping a Job and Caring for the Old*, London: NCSW.

Newcommer, Robert J. and Benton, E.F. (1978) 'Ageing and the environment', in David Hobman (ed.), *The Social Challenge of Ageing*.

P.P. (1954) *Report of the Committee on the Economic and Financial Problems of the Provision for Old Age*, Cmnd. 9333, London: HMSO.

Palo Stoller, Eleanor (1985) 'Elder–caregiver relationships in shared households', *Research on Aging* 7, 175–94.

Palo Stoller, Eleanor (1985) 'Exchange patterns in the informal support networks of the elderly: the impact of reciprocity on morale', *Journal of Marriage and the Family* 47, 335–42.

Parker, Gillian (1985) *With Due Care and Attention. A Review of Research on Informal Care*, Occasional Paper no. 2, London: Family Policy Studies Centre.

Phillipson, C.; Bernard, M.; and Straug, P. (eds) (1986) *Dependency and Independence in Old Age: Theoretical Perspectives and Policy Alternatives*, London: British Society of Gerontology.

Phillipson, C. and Walker, Alan (eds) (1986) *Ageing and Social Policy. A Critical Assessment*, Aldershot: Gower.

Pincus, Lily (1981) *The Challenge of a Long Life*, London: Faber & Faber.

Popay, Jenny and Rossiter, Chris (1982) 'Who cares about the carers?' *The Health Services* no. 31, 17.

Qureshi, H. and Walker, Alan (1986) 'Caring for elderly people: the family and the state', in C. Phillipson and Alan Walker (eds), *Ageing and Social Policy*.

Richards, Clive (1981) 'Old people and the myth of community care', *World Medicine* 16, 35–6.

Riley, Matilda White (ed.) (1979) *Aging from Birth to Death*, vol. I, AAAS Selected Symposium no. 30, Boulder, Colorado: Westview Press.

Riley, Matilda White; Abeles, Ronald P.; and Teitlebaum, M.S. (1982) *Aging from Birth to Death*, vol. II, AAAS Selected Symposium no. 79, Boulder, Colorado: Westview Press.

Ritcey, Sheila (1982) 'Substituting an interactionist for a normative model in gerontological research', *Resources for Feminist Research* 11, 220–1.

Rose, Arnold M. (1968) 'A current theoretical issue in social gerontology', in Bernice L. Neugarten, *Middle Age and Aging*, 184–9.

Rosenmayr, Leopold (1968) 'Family relations of the elderly', *Journal of Marriage and the Family* 30, 673–80.

Rosow, I. (1965) 'Intergenerational relationships: problems and proposals', in Ethel Shanas and Gordon I. Streib (eds), *Social Structure and the Family: Generational Relations*.

Seelbach, Wayne C. (1977) 'Gender differences in expectations of filial responsibility', *The Gerontologist* 17, 421–5.

Shanas, Ethel (1979) 'The family as a social support system in old age', *The Gerontologist* 19, 169–74.

Shanas, Ethel and Streib, Gordon I. (eds) (1965) *Social Structure and the Family: Generational Relations*, New York: Prentice Hall.

Shegog, R.F.A. (1981) *The Impending Crisis of Old Age: A Challenge to Ingenuity*, Oxford: Oxford University Press for the Nuffield Provincial Hospitals Trust.

Soldo, B.J. and Myllylasma, J. (1983) 'Caregivers who live with dependent elderly', *The Gerontologist* 23, 605–11.

Spreitzer, E. and Snyder, E.E. (1974) 'Correlates of life satisfaction among the aged', *Journal of Gerontology* 29, 454–8.

Stevenson, Olive (1982) 'Social trends in care for the elderly', in Frank Glendenning (ed.), *Care in the Community*.

Stiles, Jenny (1983) 'Informal care – is anyone interested in resourcing it or only in exploiting women?' *Talking Point No. 43*, 5–6.

Streib, Gordon F. and Beck, R.W. (1980) 'Older families: a decade review', *Journal of Marriage and the Family* 42, 937–56.

Taylor, Rex and Ford, Graeme (1983) 'Inequalities in old age: an examination of age, sex and class differences in a sample of community elderly', *Ageing and Society* 3, 183–208.

Thompson, L. and Walker, A.J. (1984) 'Mothers and daughters: aid patterns and attachment', *Journal of Marriage and the Family* 46, 313–22.

Thurnher, Majda (1974) 'Goals, values and life evaluations at the pre-retirement stage', *Journal of Gerontology* 29, 85–96.

Townsend, P. (1981) 'The structured dependency of the elderly: a creation of social policy in the twentieth century', *Ageing and Society* 1, 5–25.

Treas, Judith (1977) 'Family support systems for the aged. Some social and demographic considerations', *The Gerontologist* 17, 486–91.

Troll, Lillian E. (1971) 'The family of later life: a decade review', *Journal of Marriage and the Family* 33, 263–90.

Turner, Barbara F. (1979) 'The self-concepts of older women', *Research on Aging* 1, 464–80.

Wade, B.; Sawyer, L.; and Bell, J. (1983) *Dependency with Dignity*, Occasional Papers in Social Science and Administration no. 68, London: Bedford Square Press.

Walker, Alexis J. and Thompson, L. (1983) 'Intimacy and intergenerational aid and contact among mothers and daughters', *Journal of Marriage and the Family* 45, 841–50.

Walker, Alan (ed.) (1982) *Community Care: the Family, the State, and Social Policy*, Oxford: Blackwell.

Wan, T.T.H. (1982) *Stressful Life Events, Social Support Networks, and Gerontological Health*, Lexington, Mass.: Lexington Books.

Willmott, Peter with Thomas, David (1984) *Community in Social Policy*, London: PSI.

APPENDIX A

Interview schedule

This schedule was devised by the researchers to serve as a framework for the interviews. The intention was not to carry out the interviews according to a strict schedule; rather the interviewers referred to the schedule during the course of the interview to ensure that as many points as possible were covered. The schedule was also used in the process of transcribing the material.

> No.
> Date
> Time started
> Time ended
> Interviewer

PREAMBLE

[identify self, purpose of study, assure of confidentiality]

A. CARING BIOGRAPHY

Period of care

I'd like to start by finding out a bit about how long you cared for your mother.
1. For how much of your adult life did you and your mother live together?
   Always? (IF YES go to 5)
   Since _____
[If mother and daughter moved to be together:]
2. Did you visit your mother regularly before you/she moved?
3. How did you feel when you/she moved?
                              PROBE temporary, no alternative, duty, compassion, didn't want to, didn't think about future

4.   Would you take that step over again?

Why your responsibility

5.   Were there other kin or friends who might have cared for your mother?
     Who?   Brother, sister, other
6.   How did you feel about the fact that it was you who was living with mother and not them?
                         PROBE   Obligation, moral duty, altruism

Caring sequence

Now a few questions about the caring and how your mother was.
7.   When did you first feel that your mother was dependent on you?
8.   Why did your mother become dependent?
9.   Most people become more dependent as they get older. Was this the case with your mother? Please describe the turning points and significant changes.
                         PROBE   incontinence, senility, deafness, period
                                 of institutionalization or absence

Caring routines

10.   Did you get any help from:
                              emotional   practical   financial
     kin
     friends
     husband
     children
     mother
11.   Did you get any help from social services or the NHS?
                              laundry
                              home help
                              granny-sitting
                              respite care
                              nursing home
                              social work
                              day care
                              meals
                              social worker
                              aids and adaptations
                              GP
                              nurse
                    [check availability at the time]

IF NO:
Would you have liked help from social or health services?
What kind of help?
At which point in the caring period?
Did you get any help from voluntary organizations (YES/NO
Describe)

12. Did you have anyone to talk to about the problems?
IF YES: Who?

13. What was the effect of caring on your own well-being?
PROBE   health, state of mind

Mother's life

14. Did your mother go out to work at any time?
IF YES:
When?   What did she do?

15. Had your mother ever cared for another adult?

16. What were your mother's expectations for your life?

17. Did your mother have close friends?
a) before becoming dependent
b) after becoming dependent
IF YES: How often did she see them?

18. How did your mother feel about getting old?

19. How far did your mother help with the housework?

Carer's extra-caring life

I would now like to ask you a few questions about your own life while
you were caring for your mother.

20. Did you have close friends?

21. How often did you see them?

22. Did you have enough free time?
PROBE   opportunities to get away, kinds of outings, worry and guilt

23. Did you go out to work?
IF YES: When?
What did you do?

24. Did you have to give up work to care?
PROBE   decision to give up work, especially
financial considerations

25. [married women] What impact did caring for your mother have on
your family life?
PROBE   conflicts/time/routines

B. EVALUATING THE CARING PERIOD

Looking back over the time you cared for your mother, I'd like to ask a few questions about how you felt.

Relationship with mother

26. Did you feel closer as time went on?
      PROBE emotional dependency of mother/ daughter
27. Did it get easier or more difficult to talk about things as time went on?
28. Were there times when you and your mother argued?
  IF YES: PROBE about what – child-rearing? game-playing?
29. How did you feel about caring generally?
      PROBE positive feelings, e.g. of worth, love, attachment, solidarity; negative feelings, e.g. of guilt, anger
30. How did you feel about your mother's ageing?
      PROBE process of deterioration, daughter becoming mother
31. Would you have cared for anyone else like that?
32. What was most difficult about caring?
33. What was most enjoyable about caring?

Relationships with others

34. Overall, how did caring affect your friendships?
      PROBE loneliness, withdrawal, continuity
35. Overall, how did caring affect your relationship with
    a) your husband
    b) your children
    c) other kin
    PROBE children leaving home

Self

36. What expectations did you have for your life?
37. How do you feel about your own ageing?
      PROBE impact of caring on daughter, role swap: becoming like a mother
38. What advice would you give someone finding themselves about to take on the care of her mother?

C. CURRENT LIFE

I'd like to ask you a few questions about your life now.

39. What impact did your mother's death/going into care have on your life?

> PROBE routines, work, husband and children, friends, loneliness, feelings (guilt, relief, loss) missed chances

40. How have you managed to deal with the negative impacts?
41. Have you received any professional help in dealing with them?
42. What kind of care do you currently receive from social services?
43. How satisfied are you with it?
44. Would you like to see any changes in the kind of care you are receiving?

D. PREFERENCES

Generations of daughters have cared. I'd like to ask you how you feel about this in the future.

45. Under what circumstances do you think daughters should care?

> PROBE personal circumstances; with or without state aid

46. On the basis of your experience and knowledge, who do you think should bear the major responsibility of care?
47. Who should help the carer?
    Kin
    Voluntary organizations
    The state

> PROBE how – financial, cash, kind

48. [married women with daughter] Do you think your daughter will care in the same way as you have?
49. [others] Is there anyone who might care for you?
50. [those not presently being cared for] What sort of caring set-up would you like for yourself?

> PROBE informal, mixture of informal and formal (home help, day care, etc.), institutional

E. BACKGROUND

Year of birth
Marital status now
            when caring
If married: Husband: year of birth; still alive? year of death? occupation

Children: ages; marital status
Brothers and sisters: year of birth; still alive?
Race: Afro-Caribbean, Asian, white.
Education: At what age did you leave school? Further education?
Housing (now and when caring)
     privately rented
     council
     owner occupier (who is and was the owner?)
Occupation of carer: (dates)
Mother still alive?   IF YES, age; IF NO, year of death
Household composition (now and when caring)
Did you ever care for anyone else?

APPENDIX B

Caring vocabulary

ORIGINS AND GENERAL DESCRIPTION

During the course of frequent planning meetings, the researchers recognized a need to construct a 'caring vocabulary' that would serve three main purposes:

1) It would enable the researchers to be clear amongst themselves how they were perceiving their own interview material and interpreting it when transcribing the interviews.

2) It would facilitate subsequent collation and analysis of the interview material, with respect both to the project's original concern with psycho-social aspects of the mother/daughter caring relationship and to the broader field of caring literature.

3) It would contribute to the development of a framework within which caring might be understood and which would prove useful to service providers and policy-makers concerned with supporting carers and persons cared for.

The vocabulary used by the researchers was derived in a variety of ways. A term such as 'caring sequence' was used to describe the periods of differing demands on the carer's time, and these became observable only as we collected 'caring biographies'. Descriptions of the origins and development of the mother/daughter relationship as 'problematic' or 'supportive' were agreed by the researchers in the light of discussion about the interpretation of these relationships, and were essentially subjective judgements. The descriptions, broadly characterized as more-positive or more-negative, were then used as tools for examining the interrelationship of other factors in the caring process. Most of the terms we adopted to describe the process and outcome of caring were words the respondents themselves had used, unprompted, during the course of the interviews. These included phrases such as 'challenge', 'doing the right thing', and 'most worthwhile'. To complete the picture, we added some of our own, such as 'filling the gaps', and 'reluctant involvement'.

Use of these terms to describe any one set of caring relationships was by no means exclusive: combinations of terms were used to describe a relationship at any particular time, or the aftermath – 'legacy' – of caring. In order to give some sense of the ebb and flow of the caring process, we tried to examine the quality of the relationship before, at the beginning of, and at the end of the caring period. We were also conscious of the continuities, or perhaps discontinuities, in the carer's extra-caring life, and in that of the person cared for. Inputs of help and the involvement of others also varied through the course of the caring process.

We experienced some semantic difficulty in describing the person who is receiving care. In this project we could, of course, refer to the mother, and have usually done so, thereby implying 'person cared for'. When generalizing from our findings, however, we found it difficult to acknowledge the importance of personality and of social situation, as well as the physical and mental state of the person cared for. Such people are not necessarily 'patients' or 'clients'. Indeed, they are not always elderly. Research on caring has focused heavily on the needs of the carer such that a vital component of the caring matrix is in danger of being ignored, this being reflected in the absence of a suitable term to describe this person. We tried to use 'caree', but this did not seem to work very satisfactorily, so we have settled on 'person cared for'. In this way we hope to direct attention not only to the vital needs of the carer, but also to the relationship between carer and person cared for, and to the personal and emotional, as well as physical needs of the latter.

THE CARING VOCABULARY

Although it would be possible to list this vocabulary alphabetically, we feel that would diminish its use. Above all, it is intended to help clarify certain aspects of the caring process and the caring matrix (including, in this case, the mother/daughter relationship), and to enable discussion of caring as a longitudinal, fluid process.

The vocabulary thus appears under broad headings, which themselves will be defined.

How the carer came to care We identified processes which could take place at three major stages in the caring sequence; these were defined by the degree to which the carer recognized what was happening and made a conscious decision to care. The three stages at which some kind of choice, or variation in behaviour, was most possible were: coming together to live co-residentially; commencing 'semi-care' (see below); and commencing 'full care' (see below). These were points at which the carers were most likely to opt into care, or into a situation where they might face caring responsibilities in the future. It should be noted that it seemed difficult for the carer to decide to 'opt out' of caring once it had begun. Usually carers themselves were determined to see it through, and in the cases where the mother was admitted to an institution, a relative (most often husband or brother) was instrumental in insisting that co-resident caring should end.

Processes by which carers opted into care

Natural   Carers whom we described as taking on caring 'naturally' found it difficult to respond to questions about 'why you?', or 'how did you and your mother come to live together?', or 'how did you come to care?'. The word 'natural' was used unprompted by many of these respondents; caring or co-residence was seen as a natural part of their relationship. However, it could happen that while co-residence was perceived as 'natural', caring itself was regarded as more a matter of 'drift' or as a 'conscious decision'.

Drift   The phrase 'I "drifted" into it' was used by one of our respondents, and to us encapsulated the process whereby carers were gradually sucked into a timeless process to which they had given little formal consideration. Most often, a carer 'drifted' into care after a period of co-residence with the mother (which itself may have arisen from drift, or through a natural sequence of events, or a conscious decision). In these cases, the carer very often found it difficult to identify when various stages in the caring process began, as these usually developed gradually with a progressive disability such as arthritis or senile dementia.

Conscious decision   Many respondents took conscious decisions, either to live with or care for their mothers. These decisions may or may not have been willingly taken, and the roots of the subsequent positive or negative progress of the caring relationship were sometimes to be found in them; we identified some carers as having become 'reluctantly involved'. The conscious decision to care often meant that the carer had to forgo work or personal opportunities, or had to weigh up possibly conflicting needs of the mother and other members of the family. The taking of a conscious decision was often happily made; but it could also be accompanied by negative feelings about the role played by siblings, and almost always involved no consideration of the time that caring would absorb in future.

Stages in the caring sequence

The way in which the carer began co-residence and/or caring was determined in part by events that we labelled 'triggers'. These could occur at different stages in the caring sequence.

Triggers We found that many carers stressed the importance of certain life events in reporting changes in their caring biographies. Examples of these were:

1) death of father, causing children (often only children) to have to consider how they would support their mothers;

2) sudden onset of illness or disability in the mother, caused for instance by stroke or the diagnosis of cancer;

3) identifiable stage in progression of illness, such as the onset of hallucinations or violent behaviour in cases of senile dementia; or incontinence.

Such triggers often signalled new needs and new problems for the carer and person cared for, and their unpredictability illustrates the need for considering caring as a process which requires regular monitoring if appropriate action is to be taken on behalf of both parties.

Triggers were important in understanding the development of the 'caring sequence'. We found, above all, that caring was not a single process, or phase, but a collection of relationships and inputs which varied as caring progressed to its conclusion, which was reached most frequently with the death of the mother, but also with her admission to a nursing home or hospital. We identified three major stages in the caring sequence which implied different states of relationships, responsibilities, and physical and mental health, both of the carer and person cared for.

Semi-care We found that many carers felt a sense of responsibility towards their mothers even when, on the face of it, the mother's physical and mental condition did not necessarily warrant much in the way of care. In some cases, the mothers expressed a dependency: in others the daughters felt constrained by their own fears of 'what might happen' if they left their mothers. This stage could go on for years, and was usually a source of considerable constraint on the carer, often adding to a sense of weariness and 'never-endingness'. It seemed important to us to acknowledge this tie, especially when what people called 'real caring' often occupied a relatively short period of time.

Part-time full care Some respondents managed to continue working or to devote considerable time to families at the same time as bearing a full burden of care. On occasions the care was shared, with the respondent 'taking over' from a combination of informal and professional helpers on her return home from work and at weekends. It was harder to differentiate this period of care in respect to married respondents with families. But it seems that part-time full care represented a pivotal period for these women, during which caring for mothers and caring for families was held in rough balance. In contrast, during the period of semi-care the carer's efforts were devoted primarily to her own family, while in the period of full care, the balance was tipped firmly in favour of the elderly person. The main features of this type of care were the all-encompassing demands on the carer's time of paid and/or unpaid work and caring; the varying degrees of stress for the carer, depending on such things as a sympathetic response on the part of the employer and outside support; and in addition, the benefits to most carers of retaining an outside interest to balance the demands of caring.

Full care   We used this label when the mother was fully dependent and the respondent had no extra-caring ties. Obviously there were variations in the nature of the tasks performed by carers giving full care. There were sometimes triggers within this period which increased stress for carer and person cared for, such as onset of incontinence or a sudden increase in physical and/or mental incapacity. Features of full care were physical and mental stress, when most tasks were the sole responsibility of the carer; frustration; isolation; but again, satisfaction from devotion to a worthwhile task.

Within the period of full care events often occurred which contributed to changes in the nature of the caring relationship, which we turn to next.

The caring relationship

In this study, the development of the caring relationship is inextricably linked with the origins and progress of the mother/daughter relationship. We attempted to identify these as 'supportive' or 'problematic' before, at the beginning of, and at the end of the caring process. It was possible to make comparisons between the development of the relationship and other factors, such as help received, whether the respondent worked and what values she placed on work and caring, and the nature of the disability of the person cared for.

Supportive relationships   These relationships were companionate, often based on expressed love or affection between mother and daughter. Although the relationships were not necessarily egalitarian, they were mutually supportive. Each party contributed practically and/or emotionally, her contribution being valued and respected by the other. There was a minimum of manipulation or domination by either mother or daughter. These relationships could be eroded during the caring process, particularly by the mother's mental incapacity, and this often proved particularly stressful to the carer who had previously experienced a good relationship. A particularly striking feature of these relationships was the mother's 'co-operation' in her care.

Problematic relationships A few mother/daughter relationships were identified by us as being particularly problematic even before caring began. These were generally cases in which the mother had dominated or manipulated the daughter. The balance of these relationships often altered completely by the end of the caring period, with the daughter taking over the dominant role. Problematic relationships were often characterized by the mother's non-cooperation in her care, either through refusal to have anyone other than her daughter to care, or through physical or mental non-cooperation, often occasioned as much by illness as by whim. If the relationship changed its nature during the caring period, it was most likely to become increasingly problematic, with consequent stress for both daughter and mother. Indeed, the change in this relationship may well be a factor determining both mothers' and daughters' responses to offers of help.

Responses to caring

In order to co-ordinate our own perceptions of how carers had handled the caring process, we identified several types of responses by carers to caring, often using words which the carers themselves had used. It was possible for any one carer to be identified with several types of response, and the terms are useful only as a broad means of categorizing different approaches to the caring task.

Balancing act Carers often used the phrase 'balancing act' to describe the feat of organization and planning which enabled them to cope with home/family and/or job, while taking on caring. We saw different degrees of stress in balancers, ranging from those who responded to caring as a 'challenge', scheduling the day, sorting out help, and planning their work so that the task was as closely organized as possible, to those who cracked under the stress of striving to maintain normality for home and family, while meeting the demands of caring.

Immersion Some carers immersed themselves in caring to the exclusion of almost all else. For many this led to ultimate breakdown, as they shed friends, outside interests, and work to devote themselves fully to caring. For some carers this process was the only possible response to the all-encompassing nature of the caring task: without immersion the carer would not have been able to cope. For others, immersion seemed to develop gradually over time, as the outside world receded with the ever-increasing demands of caring. For this group, the apparently usual, gradual withdrawal of kin, friends, neighbours and colleagues in the face of the increasing physical and/or mental disability of the person cared for, often led to almost total isolation for the carer. This fact could easily be missed by outsiders, intent only on helping with the practical problems of disability.

Integration   The process of integrating caring into the carer's everyday life happened often by default: the carer managed to combine caring with other aspects of her life in an almost matter-of-fact way. It was likely that such carers were 'natural' carers, and that the caring was seen by them as part and parcel of the life cycle. Above all these carers achieved a balance between fulfilling their own needs and those of the person cared for, and it is interesting to note that, in the main, 'integration' was achieved when the person cared for did not suffer from mental disability and when she co-operated in her care.

These three responses describe the ways in which women sought to fit caring into their everyday lives – '*coping responses*'. We also identified *attitudinal responses* to caring:

Doing the right thing   This attitude was expressed to us many times and provided the justification for taking on the caring. It was a response common to most of our carers, who probably felt it deeply at the time of caring, perhaps because of the powerful injunction to care experienced by women. However it must be allowed that the idea may also provide a good *ex post facto* justification for the carer's commitment to the caring task.

Most worthwhile   Many carers expressed to us the feeling that caring for their mothers was one of the 'most worthwhile' things that they could do in their lives. Again, this may be part of the carer's effort to legitimize her decision to care and to reconcile herself to opportunities forgone.

Filling the gaps   This phrase was coined by us to identify those carers for whom caring seemed to fulfil a definite need in their lives, usually filling an emotional gap. This attitude towards caring could be accompanied by either more positive or more negative coping behaviours – by either integration or immersion.

The legacy of co-resident caring

The period of full care (or, very occasionally, a lengthy period of care which we designated as semi-care throughout the caring period) could end in one of two ways: with the mother's death, or with the mother's admission to nursing home or hospital. (In one case, the mother was transferred to the carer's brother's home.) The way in which a decision was made to admit the mother to an institution, and the support the carer received after the mother's transfer, could be crucial in determining these respondents' perceptions of the caring experience. The help and support which the carer and mother received in preparing for the mother's death were similarly important, as were the ways in which the respondent was able to 'pick up the pieces' when caring had ended.

Picking up the pieces The successful outcome of the caring experience depended not only on the conduct of the actual caring, but also on how well the carer was able to build a new life independent of both the caring tasks and the person cared for. The 'caring vocabulary' serves as something of a checklist for 'supporters of the supporters' when they come to consider how caring [1] as affected the carer. The length and progress of the caring sequence, quality of or changes in the caring sequence, the carer's approach to or adaptation to caring, all will have a bearing on how the carer 'picks up the pieces'. In almost all of our cases, respondents would have welcomed understanding and support in their efforts to cope with their new role once caring had ceased. Responses varied from slipping back into life with husband and family, and quickly re-achieving 'normality', to complete mental breakdown. Support and encouragement for carers picking up the pieces are vital if the costs of caring are not to be passed on to carers and their families in an unacceptable way.

APPENDIX C

Benefits for carers

Attendance Allowance is a tax free, non-means-tested benefit payable to people (over two years old, with no upper age limit of application) who require substantial help with personal needs (such as bathing, eating, toileting, dressing) because of their disabilities; *or* who require substantial supervision to avoid danger to themselves or others. The allowance is paid to a disabled person at one of two rates: the lower rate for those who require substantial care or supervision by day *or* night; and the higher rate payable to those who require care or supervision day *and* night. The benefit can be paid to people who live on their own or with others; it may be used in any way the recipient chooses, and is paid in recognition of the many extra, unavoidable expenses incurred with serious disability. Although it is paid *to* the disabled person, it may be cashed and/or spent by an assigned person other than the disabled person.

Invalid Care Allowance is a cash allowance for men and women (including female spouses only from mid-1986) who are under pension age when they commence caring for at least thirty-five hours per week for a person (who may or may not be related; who may or may not live in the same residence), who is in receipt of attendance allowance, or constant attendance allowance (under the industrial, war, or service pension schemes). The recipient must not be engaged in other paid employment which yields more than £12 a week gross. The ICA is taxable, and is assessed in means tests for other benefits. When, however, a person receives other benefit worth more than ICA, entitlement to ICA may protect the carer's state pension rights, which is an important consideration in encouraging all carers to apply for the benefit, even though their current financial position may not change.

APPENDIX D

Institutional accommodation for elderly people

RESIDENTIAL CARE

Care for elderly people who do not require extensive nursing attention can be provided in state-funded 'Part III accommodation', or in homes run either by private or voluntary concerns.

Part III of the 1948 National Assistance Act made it a duty for local authorities to provide residential accommodation for those who needed 'care and attention'. There is a minimum charge for accommodation which may be met by the social security system, and admission to Part III homes is usually restricted to those who do not own their own homes, and is allocated on a means-tested basis.

Private and voluntary organizations also provide residential care, and it is possible for some charges for this type of provision also to be met by social security, on a means-tested basis.

One of the main problems posed by residential care for carers and persons cared for in this study was that it did not normally provide nursing care, nor did it accept people who could not care for themselves, such as those with senile dementia. Some of our carers had unsuccessful experiences with residential homes for this reason. The alternative for our carers considering institutional care for their mothers thus became focused on nursing homes or hospitals.

HOSPITAL CARE

The state-funded choice for elderly people who require nursing care is usually found in a National Health Service hospital. Much hospital geriatric care is provided in large, old-fashioned wards in former, or partly run-down psychiatric hospitals. However high the quality of care, the surroundings are often depressing for patients and relatives alike.

PRIVATE AND VOLUNTARY NURSING HOMES

Subject to registration and inspection, private or voluntary organizations may set up nursing homes, and lists of these will usually be made available by local agencies to people seeking care for elderly dependants. Difficulties in finding the 'right' place, and variations in the quality of care provided caused problems for several of our respondents who chose to seek this form of care rather than use hospital-based geriatric care. Again, a proportion of costs may be met by social security in eligible cases.

INDEX

emotional: costs, 50, 152;
dependence, 52, 53; stress, *see*
stress; support, 8, 90-2, 94, 107-9,
111-12, 153, 156
employers (attitudes), 75
employment, 2, 4, 19, 38, 49; paid
work and caring, 72-7; pension
rights, 37, 74, 146; supportive
relationship and, 54-7
'enabling' support, 57, 112
EOC, 2
equal opportunities, 2, 4, 28
Ermisch, J., 1
Evandrou, M., 3, 99
Evers, H., 35, 50, 58, 59
external sources (help), 89-114

family: care, 2-4, 150-1, 153; caring for
(conflicts), 78-82; support role, 14,
30, 89, 90-2, 104, 155
fears: death, 53, 66-7;
institutionalization, 67, 98
feminine personality, 5, 21, 51, 78, 153
feminist movement, 2, 4, 5, 6, 8, 9, 15
Fengler, A.P., 73
Fennell, G., 13, 14, 29
filling the gaps, 115,159, 184
Finch, J., 6
Firth, R., 28
Fisher, L.R., 52
Forge, A., 28
formal sector, 9, 11, 100-14, 145-6;
carers' attitudes, 89, 96-9, 154-5;
partnership, 12, 154-9;
professionals, 8, 35, 154-7, 159
Fowler, N., 11, 12
friends: support role, 89, 92-5, 104,
155; *see also* social life (of carers)
full care, 83-4, 155-6, 182; caring
matrix, 135-6, 179; caring task, 32,
33-4, 39, 40, 42, 47
General Household Survey, 2, 15, 99
geriatric hospitals, 106-8, 187
Gilligan, C., 5, 6n, 153
Glendinning, C., 114
Goldberg, E.M., 11n
good neighbour scheme, 19
Goodrich, N., 73
Gorbach, P., 9, 27, 43, 45, 66, 89, 98-9,
114

government: community care
policies, 8-13; statutory services, 89,
94, 97, 98, 99-114
GPs, 90, 98, 101-3, 105, 106, 108
Graham, H., 5, 7
graphic data chart, 18-19
Groves, D., 6
Growing Older, 3, 11
guilt, 5; compulsory altruism, 6, 75; of
extra-caring life, 75, 80-1, 98; in
mother-daughter relationship,
68-70, 71, 108, 110-11

Happier Old Age, A, 11
Hareven, T.K., 17, 29
Harper, S., 1
Harrison, J., 59
Havighurst, R.J., 59
Hawley, P, 93
health deterioration, 34, 42-3, 50, 51,
68, 72, 87, 93, 152, 155
health services, 10, 89, 99-114, 187
health visitor, 100, 103
Henwood, M., 1
Hess, B.B., 22, 27, 51
home helps, 10, 65-6, 97, 103, 105
Hooyman, N., 110
hospice movement, 111
hospital care, 106-8, 187
Hubert, J., 28
Hunt, A., 2
husbands, *see* spouse

Illsey, R., 149
immersion (coping response), 115-20,
133, 183; case study, 127-31
incontinence, 42, 43-4, 46-7, 48, 69, 70,
87
informal sector, 9, 11; networks, 5, 8,
10, 31, 89, 94, 113, 149, 155;
partnership, 12, 154-9; *see also*
family; friends; neighbours
information (access), 94, 98, 100-3,
106, 108-9, 113-14, 121-2, 156
injunction to care, 5-7, 12, 27, 29, 96,
119, 138, 152-3
institutionalization, 101, 159;
accommodation types, 100, 106-8,
109-11, 114, 187; adjustment to
(carer), 71, 109-11, 119, 136-7,

Waring, J.M., 22, 27, 51
Wenger, C., 2, 29, 34, 80, 149
West, P., 149
Wicks, M., 1
widows, 28, 29, 34, 35
Wilkin, D., 92
Willmott, P., 2, 22, 34, 52, 93, 95
Wolfenden Committee, 11
women: autonomy, 18, 27, 28, 53, 64,
    71; caring (motivation), 4-7; caring

(role), 2-4, 11; feminine personality,
    5, 21, 51, 78, 153; paid work, *see*
    employment; unpaid work, 77-82;
    widows, 28, 29, 34, 35; *see also*
    mother-daughter relationship
Women and Employment Survey, 2
working class, 38

Young, M., 52